The purpose of life is to live it, to taste experiences to the utmost, to reach out eagerly and without fear for richer and newer experiences.

Eleanor Roosevelt

After reading your stories I can't help but think you remind me of Forrest Gump, not to suggest that you resemble the protagonist of that movie personally.

The Forrest Gump allusion is this idea of a "regular, ordinary guy" experiencing great events, the subtext being that the regular guy has a talent for being in the middle of things, so he himself is far from ordinary. Witnessing great events is no random accident.

On one hand, your book is a research document for our interview, but on the other, I really just want to read the book with a cup of coffee!

Tom Hale
Cinematographer, Documentarian, and Director

ANOTHER TIME

Memoir of an Ordinary Guy Growing Up during an Extraordinary Time ...the ’60s and ’70s

by Weldon Clears

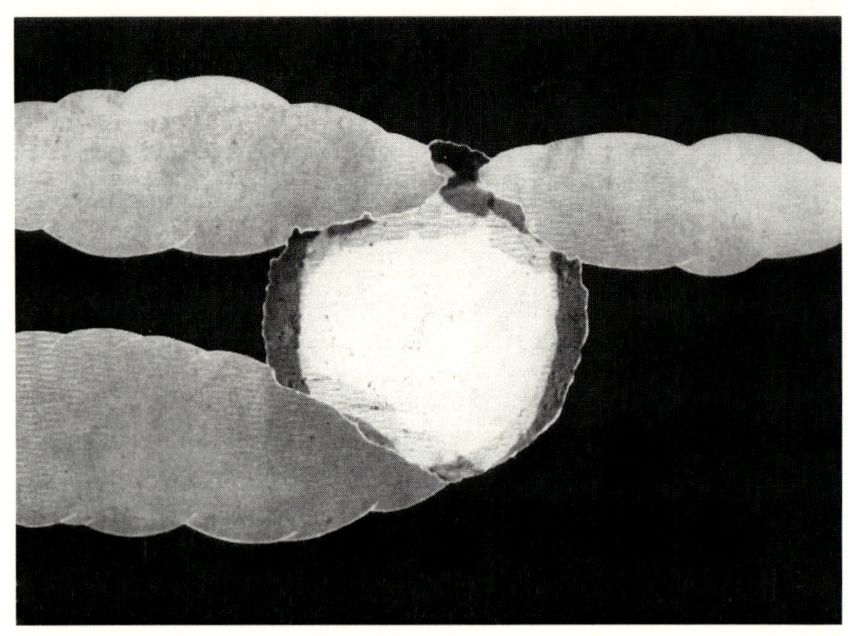

Full Moon, acrylic on canvas 4' x 6'

Back cover artwork:
Soho Market on Thompson Street, 30" x 24" pastel,
Canson Mi-Teintes 1976
Flatiron Building, NYC, 24" x 30" color pencils,
Canson Mi-Teintes 1978
Pink Sphinx, 24" x 30" pastel, Canson Mi-Teintes, 1974
USA, 5' x 8' oil on canvas 1978

Copyright © 2018-2021 Weldon Clears.
All rights reserved.

ISBN: 978-0-692-85866-0 (Paperback)
ISBN: 978-0-578-24835-6 (eBook)

Acknowledgements

Thanks to everyone who made me think that several of my experiences were interesting enough to write about.

Special thanks to my good friends Barbara and Mark White for helping me transfer my thoughts and photos.

To my long-time friend Poki Olson, the best graphic designer I've ever met, who designed the cover.

To Patti, Amanda, and Allison, my eternal gratitude for listening to me tell these stories over and over again.

The generous contributions you've all made to this book make it even more special.

Table of Contents

Mom, Dad, brother Arthur, Brownie, and our 1959 Rambler Ambassador

Graduation, 1965, Division Avenue High School

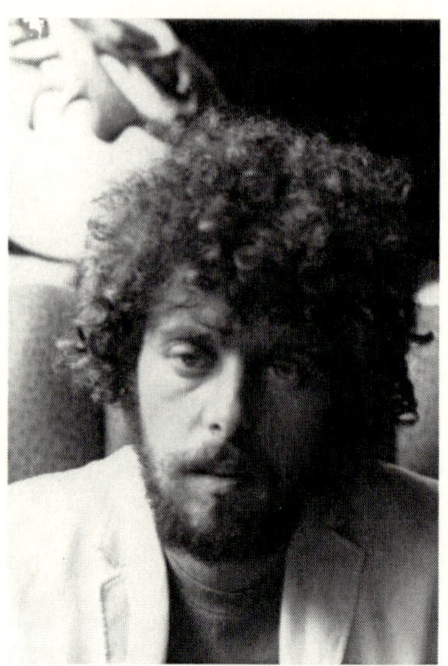
Several years later

Preface

Some of my most interesting and formative years were during the '60s and '70s. It was a very tumultuous time, and it was an amazing time.

The following stories are told to the best of my recollection. Some of the dates might be off, and some of my friends who were part of these stories might be missing, and to that I say I'm sorry. Remember, some of these events happened forty to fifty years ago. Sometimes I have problems remembering what I did yesterday.

I had what I thought was an ordinary family life growing up in Levittown, L.I. It was somewhat white-bread. But everything changed when I graduated from high school. Because of the extraordinary times and the people I met, I experienced things I never thought I would.

Everyone is offered opportunities and chances. You can take them or leave them. I chose to take some of them, and they became adventures and experiences.

One
Introduction

Background

Family

I was born at Doctors Hospital in New York City in 1947. We lived in Brooklyn until I was five, when we moved to Levittown, Long Island. When we moved there, I thought we had moved to the country, even though we were only 45 minutes from New York City. The houses were all virtually the same. They were small one-floor houses, 900 square feet with an unfinished expansion attic. Each one had two bedrooms, one bathroom, a kitchen, and a living room. Ours was brown with white shutters and white trim.

One of the best things about living in Levittown was that there were swimming pools within blocks of where I lived. In the summer I went to the pool with my buddies every day. Another great thing was Halloween. Every house had kids, so all of the families celebrated it. I was able to fill two shopping bags full of candy. I usually dressed up like a hobo.

I went to St. Bernard's Church, where I received my First Communion and Confirmation.

Animals

We always had a dog. Skippy, Tippy, Brownie, and Oliver were members of our family at different times. All of them were lovable mutts.

Mom (Dora)

Upon arriving in New York City from Naples, Italy, my mom and her sisters and brothers settled in Brooklyn. Her father was a builder, and her mother took care of all the kids. My mom lived with them until she got married to my dad.

My mom loved her family and cooking. Any time my friends came over, she'd make them sit down to eat something she had made. They never complained. We never ordered in, and the only time we went to a restaurant was on Mother's Day or Father's Day. Mom had a beautiful complexion that people always complimented her on. Once we got settled in Levittown, she worked at different factories on Long Island.

Dad (Arthur)

My dad's heritage was English, and he was born in San Francisco. When he turned eighteen, he moved to Brooklyn and drove an armored truck. When he wasn't working, he'd be down at the Sheepshead Bay dock working on his fishing boat, the *Tarpon*, that he chartered.

After we moved, he still loved going fishing. In the summer, we'd go fishing every other Saturday. He would wake my brother and me up at 5:30 a.m. Although we really wanted to go, we always complained about getting up so early. While we got dressed, he prepared our lunch. By 6 a.m. he had made our lunches, loaded our fishing poles and reels and an outboard motor into the car.

He'd drive to Babylon, on the south shore of Long Island, where he rented a boat. It was sixteen feet long and came with an anchor, oars, and three life vests. He'd attach the outboard motor to the transom, buy some bait, and then we'd head out into the Great South Bay. We would go from spot to spot. We did the same routine all day.

We were happy to catch anything. Although we fished for flounders or flukes, we usually caught blowfish. It didn't matter because it was so much fun. Years later he bought a boat with a trailer, and we travelled all over the island and launched it at different locations.

He was also a handy guy. He always seemed to have a project to work on. One time he built our garage; another time he built two rooms in our attic.

Brother (Arthur)

Arthur was four years older than me, which is a big gap when you're young. He had a great laugh and was a very enterprising guy. He was always looking for a way to make money. He delivered *Newsday*, a local Long Island newspaper, when he was a teenager. When he quit, I took over his route, and by getting over fifty new subscribers, I became an honor carrier and went to Camp Newsday.

After he stopped delivering newspapers, he started a landscape business while also working in a pharmacy. With the money he made he traveled and bought cars. From 1964 to 1979, he had an MGA, a Chevrolet Corvair, a Chevrolet Nova, a Chevrolet Chevelle (our neighbor was a Chevrolet dealer), and a Pontiac Bonneville. After college he became an elementary school teacher. Years later when he moved to San Francisco, he became a principal.

Gramps (Arthur)

My paternal grandfather grew up in London and went to Uxbridge and then to Oxford. He was a very smart and industrious man. After he graduated from Oxford, he and his brother bought two jewelry stores in London. After a few years, they sold their stores, and my grandfather moved to San Francisco, where my dad was born. After my dad grew up, my grandfather moved to Wheeling, West Virginia. I'm not sure why or what he did there. He never talked about my grandmother, and when he moved to Virginia, she didn't go with him.

Once he got settled, he bought some land on a farm near a river and built a houseboat. Every summer, we'd visit him for a week. We'd drive down there in our Hudson Commodore.

Some days we played with the kids that lived on the farm just down the road, and some days we'd go out in my grandfather's rowboat and fish or catch crabs or dig for clams.

Living on a houseboat was different and fun. The only problem was going to the bathroom. He had an outhouse that stunk. It was about fifty feet from the house, and at night it was scary, at least for me.

When he turned eighty, living alone on a houseboat became too difficult, so my parents had him move in with us.

Every day he wore a suit with a tie and a vest no matter how warm it was. Every morning he'd wake up at six o'clock and walk the dog. After walking the dog he'd come home and have a hot toddy, whiskey and tea. The rest of the day he'd spend reading the newspaper and doing the crossword puzzle.

School

I went to Summit Lane Elementary school that was about five blocks away. Every morning I'd meet my friends on the corner and walk to school. There were about twenty-five kids in each class. There was nothing special about the teachers or the curriculum. I still have a friend, Doug, that I met in third grade.

The junior/high school, Division Avenue High School, was a block away. There were several hundred kids in our graduating class.

It had the usual bullies who would pick on me. Having a name like Weldon made me a perfect target. I guess my parents wanted to be a little creative by naming me that, especially since my grandfather, father, brother, and uncle had the same name. There were the usual cute girls and cheerleaders who made me feel like I was invisible, and some days I wished I were. I tried fitting in by playing soccer and wrestling, but that didn't work too well. I never felt like I fit in or could be myself, although I wasn't sure what that was.

Two
The '60s and '70s

Just imagine: you're in high school getting ready to graduate, going into the "real world," and everything in the world starts changing. Things that I never imagined were happening.

During the '60s, John Kennedy, Martin Luther King Jr., Malcolm X, and Robert Kennedy were assassinated. The Civil Rights movement was gaining support. So was the women's equal rights movement. Many women burned their bras to show their support, and the demonstrations against the war in Vietnam were getting larger. There were demonstrations, sometimes riots, and marches for all of them. Students were protesting on campuses and in every city.

We almost got into a war with Russia over an incident called the Cuban Missile Crisis, and we walked on the moon. It was an unbelievable time.

Society

There were new words and phrases that became popular: make love not war, turn on tune in drop out, free love, groovy, far out, psychedelic, hippies, acid, lava lamps, pong.

Fashion

Women started wearing pants, bikinis, granny glasses, miniskirts, bell-bottom and elephant bell-bottom pants. They cut their hair short in a style called the pixie cut. Go-go boots – white boots with low heels and mid-calf in height – were popular.

Men started wearing their hair long. Guys wore shirts with ruffles. Tie-dye became popular. A method of producing textile patterns by tying parts of the fabric to shield it from dye, it created unique designs on shirts and pants. Paisley prints, using a teardrop design, were popular. Leather fringe on jackets and pants became the rage. Guys wore Beatle boots made popular by the Beatles, ankle-high boots with a sharp, pointed toe with either elastic or zippers on the sides. Anything that was colored red, white, and blue was popular.

Drugs

Acid (LSD), barbiturates, amphetamines, cocaine, hashish, Quaaludes and marijuana.

Music

There was the British invasion: the Beatles, Rolling Stones, Led Zeppelin, the Who, the Zombies, Ten Years After, and many more. It seemed that there was a new band from England coming to the United States every week.

American musicians became popular: Bob Dylan, Jack Elliott, Joan Baez, Judy Collins, Richie Havens, Arlo Guthrie, the Byrds, Santana, Jefferson Airplane, James Brown, the Eagles, and the Beach Boys.

The Motown sound: Diana Ross & the Supremes, Smokey Robinson & the Miracles, Stevie Wonder, the Temptations, the Four Tops, Marvin Gaye, Michael Jackson & the Jackson 5, Martha Reeves and the Vandellas, and numerous other groups.

The punk movement started in New York City in the '70s with The Ramones, the New York Dolls, the Heartbreakers, Richard Hell and the Voidoids, Television, The Velvet Underground, Patti Smith, and the Senders.

Later in the '70s disco was popular.

Sports

There were several outstanding things that happened in sports, but the position taken by Muhammad Ali, the heavyweight champion, stands out as the only one that was influenced by the times. He refused to serve in the army, citing his religious beliefs and opposition to America's involvement in Vietnam. He was banned from boxing for three years, and during this time, he changed his name from Cassius Clay to Muhammad Ali.

Besides being an incredible boxer and the man who invented the "rope-a-dope," he was a poet. Sometimes he'd write a poem prior to his match. "I should be a postage stamp. That's the only way I'll ever get licked." Some poems predicted how the match would turn out: "If he doesn't want more, I'll end it in four."

Art

The art world was also changing; Pop Art, Op Art, Minimalism, Neo-Expressionism, and Abstract Expressionism were born. New York City, specifically Soho, became the capital of the art world. Andy Warhol, Jasper Johns, Roy Lichtenstein, Robert Rauschenberg, Donald Judd, James Turrell, and later Jean-Michael Basquiat became household names.

Three
Working at Jones Beach

Kids in high school or college usually have summer jobs, and in the spring of my junior year in high school, I got one at Jones Beach at $1.25 an hour. Years later, the money I made paid for college. It was an ideal job – I was getting paid to go to the beach and get a tan.

I always started working there in June, when school was over. Every morning I'd leave my parents' house, walk about a quarter of a mile to the Wantagh Parkway, and hitch a ride to the beach. Several years later I got there on my motorcycle.

All summer help wore the same uniform: grey pants, a gray pullover v-neck shirt, and a white gob navy hat. In the beginning of the season I was assigned a field to work at. Each field had a little office where we took our breaks when we weren't cleaning the beach. There were two shifts. I always worked the day shift.

The guys that cleaned the beach were called paper-pickers. I was one of those guys. Most times, after I changed into my uniform we would line up the baskets on the beach and then walk up and down the beach with a long stick that had a trigger by the grip that we used to pick up paper cups, candy wrappers, newspapers, and anything else that wasn't supposed to be on the beach. We carried dark green canvas bags slung over our shoulders that we put the garbage in. Occasionally, besides picking up garbage I would try to pick up girls, although I wasn't too successful. By the middle of the summer, everyone that worked there had a good tan.

After a couple of years of doing that, I heard about another job that paid more. This new job was on the pool crew and paid $1.75 an hour. The pool crew consisted of five guys including a manager. We'd start at four a.m. vacuuming the Olympic-size pool first, and then we'd vacuum the baby pool at the West Bathhouse. Some days we'd luck out and find money. We started working that early so that we were done at nine when the pool opened. After taking a break we'd sweep the area outside of the pool, and we finished at one p.m.

Besides working at Jones Beach, I played on the employees' softball team as a pitcher. It was high-arc pitching. The lifeguards were our toughest competitors. Our team was good and won the championship four out of six years.

Jones Beach was a special place. While working there I met and lived with some of the nicest guys that I still know: Joel, Rich, Pat, Mike, Bobby, Larry, Peter, Glen, JJ, and Tom.

Newport Folk Festival

One July morning while I was working, my friend Glen, who also worked at Jones Beach as the ambulance driver, asked me if I'd like to join him and his friend and go to the Newport Folk Festival. I had never heard of it, but it sounded like fun, so I said, "Yes." Glen got tickets for three days. The following week we drove up there in his 1965 Buick Riviera (tan interior, forest green exterior, convertible), a beautiful car.

The Newport Folk Festival was the first music festival I had ever gone to. It was a great experience, and it also became one of the pivotal moments in folk music. Bob Dylan was there and went electric. Unfortunately, we didn't see his show, but who knew he was going electric? We would have tried a lot harder to get tickets if we had known.

Once we got there, instead of renting a motel room, we decided to sleep in the town park along with hundreds of other people. There were young people hanging out all over town; it was a "happening." When we weren't at the festival, we walked around town or hung out in the park. In the morning before breakfast we'd either wash up at a fountain in the park or at a gas station. We'd have breakfast at a diner in town and then go to the festival. We saw Pete Seeger, Judy Collins, Theodore Bikel, Joan Baez, and Peter, Paul and Mary.

It seemed as if at least a third of the people who were in the park played guitars. When I went to sleep and when I woke up, there was always someone playing their guitar, singing, dancing, or getting high. Everyone in the park was friendly and became our temporary friends. It was a unique experience sleeping outside in a park with strangers.

Four
Graduation from High School

After graduating from high school, all my friends went to college, but I didn't, not at first. My parents said it was up to me to decide what I wanted to do with my life, so I continued to live with them. Most days I stayed in my room in the attic, listening to music and reading. I listened to all the new English and American groups, even jazz. Someone told me to listen to Miles Davis – "he'll blow your mind" – which he did. I thought maybe the secret of what I should do with my life was in music. I didn't have any direction, but it wasn't long before that changed.

One day while I was sitting around doing nothing, I received a letter from my draft board. It said, "Congratulations, you have been chosen to serve your country in the United States Armed Forces." I was scheduled to take a physical exam. I was skinny but healthy and wasn't worried about passing, which I thought was the goal, but years later, passing the physical was the last thing I wanted to do.

The draft board had a bus waiting for me and several other guys that took us to Fort Hamilton for the physical exams. I passed.

A soldier who was signing everyone out said to me, "You'll probably get another notice from your draft board soon, for a second and final physical. Expect to be drafted." He also said, "You should beef up and gain some weight before returning." I weighed 118 pounds.

A few days later, while I was watching the news, the government announced that they were going to increase the number of troops in Vietnam. That's when it hit me. If I got drafted, that's probably where I would go. Going to Vietnam wasn't something I wanted to do, so I decided to change my availability, by going to college and getting a student deferment.

Five
College

I applied to Nassau Community College a couple of days later since it was close to where I lived. I got accepted to night school and began classes in the spring of 1966.

The first person I met at night school was Steve Shevlin. One night, when the professor gave us a break, Steve asked me, "Do you want to double-date with me and my girlfriend and see the Rolling Stones at Forest Hills Stadium?" You bet. The Stones were my favorite band.

From that point on I knew he and I would become good friends. The following year I started going to Nassau Community College full time, and so did he.

My draft classification was now 2S. Registrant deferred because of activity in study.

After a year and a half at NCC I transferred to Hofstra University, and so did Steve. He and I continued to be best friends, and when he got married, I was his best man. Since we were both art majors, we had many of the same classes. We also did several other things together outside of school.

We started a leather business, boxed, participated in several demonstrations, worked at various jobs for Manpower, a temporary hiring agency and drove taxi cabs in Manhattan.

The following stories are about some of the things we did. Also during this time, the war in Vietnam was growing, and keeping a student classification became a constant challenge for me and thousands of other students.

Six
S & W Leather

One summer day Steve came by my parents' house, where I was still living. We talked about what we were doing. He said that he was earning money by making and selling leather belts, sandals, and wristbands. He said, "It seems that anything I make out of leather sells. I'm not making much money, but I'm doing alright." He asked me, "Do you want to help me? If you did, we could make more stuff and hopefully make more money than I'm making now." I told him, "I'd like to, but I'm working at Jones Beach and don't have the time."

When fall came and classes started, Steve asked me again. "Now that you're not working at the beach, maybe you'd like to help me expand my leather business?" I had the time, so I decided to give him the money he needed to grow his business, and I became his partner and assistant. He was happy to get the additional money and felt that this arrangement would work. So did I.

He had a shop set up in his parents' basement with a bench, a shelf for dyes, buckles, and a place for the leather. When we needed to replenish our supplies, we'd go to lower Manhattan and buy large leather skins or snake skins that we used to cut into strips to make belts. Sometimes we'd dye them red, white, and blue. Our red, white, and blue belts and snakeskin belts sold very well. We also made three- and five-braided wristbands and pants.

Some days, before going to school we'd put on two or three belts that we had made the previous night. Before class started or when we were in the cafeteria, we'd show the other students our belts by lifting our shirts. It was a little weird to do, but we got sales.

Besides selling our goods at Hofstra, we expanded and started selling our stuff in several head shops on Long Island and in Queens. We did our best sales in a store our friend Richie owned called "Instant Pants," on Queens Boulevard in Forest Hills. He sold jeans and hippie tie-dye clothing, so our leather stuff fit right in.

Almost all the money we made went back into the business, although we did use a few bucks for gas, food, and socializing.

As if the experience and money weren't gratifying enough, we were able to use this business for our senior project. We submitted a detailed business plan, samples of our merchandise, and stationery with our company's name and logo. The company was called S & W: Steve & Weldon. Tricky name, huh? We both got A's on the project.

Seven
Boxing

I had just got home from working at the beach one day when Steve came over. We sat around listening to music and talking about our summer. I was telling him how well the employee softball team that I played on was doing.

I asked him, "Are you into sports?"

He said, "I box."

I was surprised to hear this and asked, "You box?"

He said, "I have a manager and a trainer, and belong to the Mid Island A.C. gym, where I train."

I couldn't believe it. Steve didn't look like a boxer. He was thin and had long hair. Since I had never boxed and had never been in a boxing gym, I asked him if I could go with him the next time he worked out. "Maybe I could box you?"

"Sure. I'm going to the gym tomorrow."

Little did I know this would be an experience that would lead to opportunities I would never forget.

The next day he picked me up, and we drove to his gym in Brentwood, Long Island. It was in a small building and had a boxing ring, a heavy bag, a speed bag, a mat, and a couple of jump ropes hanging on a hook. It smelled of sweat. In the back were lockers, but it didn't have a shower.

Steve introduced me to his trainer, Gene. He was about five-foot ten and weighed about two hundred and eighty pounds.

Gene wanted to know why I was there.

I told him, "I'm going to box Steve."

"Do you know how to box?"

"No, but I'm athletic and play softball at Jones Beach," as if that mattered.

He smiled and then punched me in my solar plexus, knocking me to the floor. Anyone who's been hit in their solar plexus knows that your breath gets knocked out of you and your eyes start to tear.

I looked up from the floor, completely surprised by what had just happened, and while struggling to catch my breath, I said, "Are you fuckin' crazy!"

Gene smiled and helped me up. While I was wiping away my tears, he said, "Stevie will do a lot worse to you."

Over the next couple of years, I learned that Gene was a great guy but a little wacky, and he did unexpected things like that.

Anyway, I was so mad that I couldn't wait to get into the ring and prove Gene wrong. I would take my anger out on Steve.

Gene gave me a pair of boxing shorts, a very well-padded jock, headgear, a large mouthpiece, and shoes. Then he tied sixteen-ounce gloves on me. Some people call sixteen-ounce gloves "pillows," but I learned that getting hit with these pillows was anything but soothing.

After changing I climbed into the ring. Gene rang the bell. I ran over to Steve and started hitting him with wild swings. He pushed me back and kept me away with jabs. After the bell rang, Gene asked me, "Have you had enough?" I hadn't.

The next round, we moved around the ring, but this time I tied him up by grabbing his arms, so that he couldn't throw any more jabs. Then I started hitting him in his liver, which wasn't right and not legal in boxing. He got pissed. He pushed me back, and as I stepped towards him, he hit me with an uppercut. I went down. It was the first time I saw stars.

Gene jumped into the ring with a grin on his face and said, "I told you." He helped me up, threw some water on my face, and asked me, "Do you want to learn how to box?"

From that day on, Gene and Steve's manager Freddie, whom I met later, became my trainer and my manager as well as my friends.

We'd go to the gym four or five days a week. One day when we were working out, Gene told us that Freddie and Rocky Graziano were good friends. "They boxed together when they were in the Marines."

Freddie had never mentioned that or his fights. He talked about a lot of things, like his family, but not much about himself. Freddie was a tough guy but also one of the nicest guys you could meet. He was one of those guys that if you were in a fight, you'd want him on your side. He was not someone you'd want to mess with.

I liked Freddie and looked forward to the times he would jump into the ring and work with me. What an experience. He worked on my hand speed and showed me how to throw punches and how to knock down punches. Sometimes, when I dropped my hands, he'd hit me fairly hard. He said, "It's the best way to remember to keep your hands up."

Some days we'd spar with the other guys, but most days Steve and I would spar with each other. Gene worked on our footwork and the various punches: hooks, uppercuts, jabs, and body shots. Afterwards, we'd work on the speed bag and the heavy bag, and skip rope.

Gene toughened up our abs by having us lie down on a mat and then throwing a ten-pound medicine ball at our stomachs, two reps ten times. After a while I could take body shots. Sometimes Steve and I thought he threw the medicine ball a lot harder than necessary, but that was Gene.

There were boxing gyms all over Long Island and Queens that showcased their fighters. The matches were called "smokers." They were open to the public and usually held at various boxing gyms, high school gyms, or large conference rooms in hotels. They were usually held on Friday nights, with six to eight bouts a night.

After a few months I was good enough to fight in these smokers. The hard work paid off.

Bleeding

My biggest problem when I boxed was that my nose would bleed when I was hit with a good punch, usually a straight right. Gene called me a "bleeder." He said, "There are a few ways to stop that. You could work on not getting hit, or you could get your nose cauterized by a doctor – but that costs money – or you could sniff in salt water to toughen the inside of your nose."

Since I didn't have money for a doctor, I decided to start sniffing salt water, along with getting better at knocking down punches, and bobbing and weaving. Every night after returning from the gym, I'd pour a little salt into the palm of my hand, add a little warm water, and sniff it in. It burned like hell. Of course, my mom and dad thought I was crazy and suggested that if I wanted to stop the bleeding, I should stop boxing. Why didn't I think of that?

If I knew I had a fight coming up, I'd do it two or three times a day. It worked, and I didn't bleed for a few fights. Unfortunately, it didn't always work, and when it didn't, the ref would stop the fight even though I wasn't hurt and wanted to continue. It's called a TKO (technical knockout). What a drag.

Bleeding wasn't the only physical thing I experienced. One fight I got hit with a good hook on the side of my head, right on my ear, that broke my eardrum. I didn't know it had happened until I realized that the ref and Gene's voices sounded muffled. It took a couple of months before my eardrum healed.

Sometimes after going to the gym, if we had sold some belts, we'd go to Steve's parents' house to make more. If we were lucky, his mom was home, and she'd make us sandwiches. She made the best sandwiches. After eating we'd go downstairs and make some belts, wristbands, or anything we thought would sell. We'd do that for a few hours, and then I'd go home.

Most mornings, since Steve and I had the same schedules, he'd pick me up in his 1960 blue Chevy with the shift on the steering column, and we'd go to school. The deal was that he'd drive, and I'd pay for gas. Gas was only twenty-eight cents a gallon. Sometimes the gas stations would have a gas war, and the price was even less.

Some mornings, Gene would pick us up before school and drive us to a local high school track to do roadwork.

Over the years Gene would occasionally tell us that we were changing gyms. We never knew why, and it didn't matter. All of them were on Long Island: Northport, Bay Shore, Freeport, and they were all the same, with a small boxing ring, a heavy bag and a speed bag, and the same smell: sweat mixed with antiseptic cleanser.

Golden Gloves

One afternoon Gene told us that he had entered us in the Golden Gloves, a competition sponsored by the *New York Daily News*. I had heard about the Golden Gloves, but I never thought I'd be in it.

I was excited. I couldn't imagine training any harder, but I did. In between sessions of my homework I'd do sit-ups and work out with weights. Some days I'd go to the high school track a block away and do roadwork. I had been boxing in smokers every few weeks and was winning, so I felt confident that I could do well. I was in the bantamweight class, 118 pounds.

Gene and Freddie were also confident I'd do well. Most of the guys in my weight class were shorter and had shorter reaches, which made my jab much more effective.

The match was at St. Raymond's High School in the Bronx. I was nervous and excited.

Gene picked me and Freddie up. Freddie lived in East Meadow, a town next to Levittown. He also picked up another guy who was fighting that night. On the way to the fight Gene was telling us how well we'd do. He told me to be aggressive and, with my reach, to use my jab a lot.

The gym was packed. When I signed in, we found out whom I was fighting. After Gene and Freddie heard whom I was fighting, their tone and advice changed.

I changed into my good-luck shorts, which were white with a black stripe on each side, and my boxing shoes, which were black. After changing, I joined Gene and Freddie and started to warm up, doing some stretching and shadow-boxing.

As I was warming up, they reminded me to protect myself and to keep moving. Freddie said, "Don't forget to bob and weave and knock down his punches and keep your hands up. If you start bleeding, tie the guy up." They changed their advice from being aggressive to being defensive. I sensed that they knew the guy I was fighting, and it wasn't good for me.

Fifteen minutes later they called me and the other guy. As I walked into the gym, everyone was yelling and stomping their feet.

My opponent was a wiry black guy about three inches taller than me. There went my reach advantage.

After the ref told us the rules, we went back to our corners. Once the bell rang, we immediately started throwing punches in the middle of the ring. I was hitting him with some good jabs and some good body shots. He was taking my punches while also throwing some powerful punches himself.

After the first round Gene said I probably won the round. The second round I continued to be careful, but then I got hit with a good right and my nose started bleeding. I tried doubling up on my punches and wobbled him with a couple of good combinations. I was hoping to knock him out before my bleeding became an issue. Gene thought the second round was a draw, but he didn't know how much my bloody nose would influence the judges. Freddie did a great job of stopping the bleeding. They both suggested that I better end this fight as soon as I could. That sounded like a good idea.

As soon as the bell rang, we stood head and toe exchanging punches. I was bobbing and weaving, knocking down his punches while also getting some good body shots in, but then he hit me with another good right, and I started bleeding again. As I was trying to wipe the blood away from my eyes, I got hit with another right. As I was going down, he continued to hit me until the ref stepped in.

I got up by the count of four, but my nose was bleeding a lot. I looked worse than I felt, but the ref called the match. Another TKO but this time it was the Golden Gloves. I was depressed. It was frustrating losing because my nose bled. The other fighter from our gym won his fight.

On the way home Gene and Freddie told me that the guy I fought had been fighting for several years and was a tough fighter who would probably win the weight class…He did.

Although I was disappointed about losing, there was one consolation. The next morning, when Steve picked me up for school, he showed me a copy of the *Daily News*. In the sports section there was a photograph of me getting knocked down with the other fighter still trying to hit me. And the following day the *Daily News* had another picture of me, this time with me getting hit with a jab. Although I felt cool seeing my picture in the *Daily News* sports section, I would have rather won.

Turning Pro

A month after the Golden Gloves, maybe because I was constantly sniffing in salt water, and maybe because of all the training with Gene and Freddie, I was getting hit a lot less, and when I was hit, my nose rarely bled. I started winning fights, some by knockouts.

One day, on the way to the gym, Steve said, "I think I'm going to turn pro." He was doing well, so I wasn't surprised to hear this.

That night I couldn't stop thinking that maybe I could also turn pro. For the next two weeks I couldn't get this thought out of my head.

What would that be like? I knew I didn't have the experience or the number of fights many fighters have before they turn pro, so I asked Gene and Freddie what they thought. They said, "Maybe you want to wait and get a few more matches under your belt."

For the next several months I fought as often as I could. Finally, one day I told them that although I respected their opinions, I wanted the opportunity to fight professionally.

First Pro Fight

One day when I arrived at the gym, Freddie said, "Hey, kid, I got you your first pro fight in Secaucus, New Jersey, in a few weeks." Super.

We decided that after that fight, we'd reassess my continuing as a pro.

I was thrilled. I was ready. I did a lot of road work and was going to the gym six days a week.

Finally, the day of my fight arrived. I didn't go to school. Instead, Gene, Freddie, and Elliot, a middleweight from the gym who was also fighting that night, picked me up, and we drove to the weigh-in. The weigh-in was at some office in the city at noon. After the weigh-in we went to a diner and had lunch. Then we went back to the gym. I did some homework while Gene and Freddie worked with some of the other fighters. My match was scheduled for 7:00 p.m.

As Gene drove to the arena, Freddie, who was a very positive guy, kept telling Elliot and me how well we'd do. I can still hear him say, "Keep moving. Keep throwing your jab, and when he lets down his guard, drop your right in." They knew whom I was fighting and felt that this was a good test for me. I wasn't worried about fighting that night, but I was worried about bleeding.

Rocky Graziano

On the way to the fight Freddie asked Gene to pull over so he could make a phone call. When he returned, he said that he just spoke to Rocky, who said he was going to be in the area and that he'd drop by the fight.

As we pulled into the parking lot, we knew that Rocky was already there. There was a huge crowd surrounding someone. It had to be Rocky, and it was.

When we got out of the car, Freddie and Gene walked over to him and gave him a big hug. Freddie introduced Elliot and me to him. What a thrill! They filled him in on who we were fighting and at what time.

As we walked into the arena, Rocky put his arm around my shoulder and said, "Don't worry, kid, you'll do good." I'll never forget that moment.

I couldn't wait to fight. Not only did I want to win for myself, but also for Gene, Freddie, and now Rocky.

The locker room was small and smelled. Elliot and I had lockers next to each other. After I got dressed, Gene wrapped my hands. Typically wraps are thin strips of cloth that are wrapped around your hands and fastened with tape, which go on before you put on your gloves. Since I was going to fight before Elliot, I started to warm up.

Finally, they called my name and said, "You're next." As we walked out of the locker room, I saw the arena was filled. The other guy was already in the ring and seemed to have a lot of fans who were calling his name.

The fight was four rounds. After I climbed into the ring I went to my corner. Gene had my mouthpiece, and after rinsing it off, he put it in my mouth. They announced to the crowd who was fighting, and everyone started cheering and whistling. The ref called us to the middle of the ring and explained the rules. The bell rang, and we both moved around trading punches, measuring each other out.

Gene thought the first round was a draw. The second round probably went to him. He hit me with some good body shots. Gene and Freddie were yelling at me to move and to jab more. In the third round we were trading punches, and he dropped me with an uppercut followed by a left hook. I got up and was saved by the bell. He won that round.

The fourth round I knew I had to be much more aggressive and try to knock him out. He was taking my punches. We both traded some good shots, and I was glad my nose wasn't bleeding. But I "spoke" too soon. He hit me with a good combination, and my nose started bleeding profusely. He then started throwing everything he had, and I did the same. There was blood on me, on him, and on the ref when he tried to separate us.

I was having trouble seeing and got hit with a good hook. I went down. I got up at the count of five, but the ref stopped the fight, two minutes, twenty seconds into the fourth round. TKO.

While I was changing into my street clothes, this guy came over to me and gave me fifty dollars, saying, "That's for the fight. Thanks."

I had no doubt what I would do with it. The only right thing to do was give it to Gene and Freddie. After Elliot's fight, which he won, I walked over to them and thanked them for all the work they had done in preparing me for this fight and gave them the money. They told me to keep it. I knew they'd say that, but I told them that I felt that I owed them a lot more than just fifty bucks and insisted they take it. Freddie said, "Rocky left after your fight, but he told me to wish you good luck."

I decided to take a break from boxing after that. I was trying to figure out if I wanted to continue. I also saw a nose doctor who said that cauterizing my nose would be helpful but, sooner or later, with a couple of good punches, it'd probably start bleeding again.

I decided to quit. I gave it a lot of thought, but the reality was that, being a bleeder, I'd never be the fighter I wanted to be. I also knew I wasn't willing to put in the time to find out how good I could be, and I didn't want to waste Freddie or Gene's time.

It was a great experience. I thank Steve for turning me on to boxing and for introducing me to Gene and Freddie and having them in my corner.

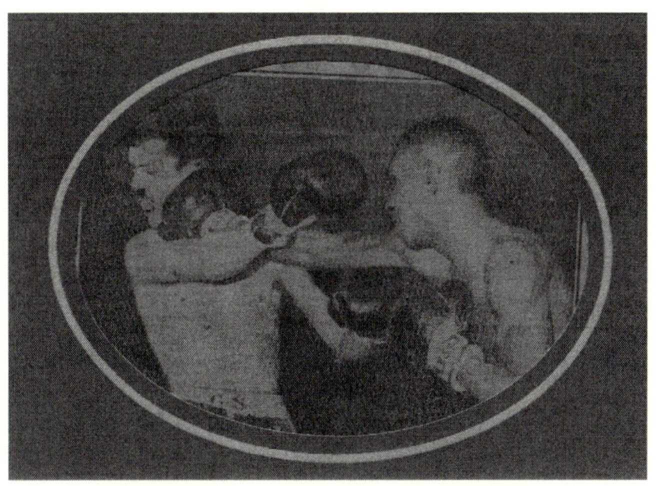

DECEMBER 22, 1966 ● 22

Mike Lee Reports

STRONG GOLDEN GLOVES TEAM

The Mid Island A.C. of Islip Town is putting together a strong Golden Gloves contingent . . . Fred Menna's gym at 256 Orinoco Dr., Brightwaters, is buzzing with young fighters anxious to make good in amateur fisticuffs . . . the team has two of the finest coaches in the Met area in Patrolman Joe Thomas of the Suffolk Police, a former Navy champion, and Gene Moore, who trained Elliott Miller when the latter won the 160-pound Golden Glove title in 1965.

Fine prospects in the open class are Earl Woods, 126-pounder from Brentwood; Carlos Marchand, a nice looking lightweight; Jose Ortiz, hard-punching welterweight from Brentwood, and Miles Cuffy, who punches with authority.

In the sub-novice division, the Mid-Island group has a strong group headed by Irish Buddy Black, 215-pound heavyweight who made All-Suffolk while playing end for Central Islip's undefeated teams; Dave Petis and Joe McCluskey, ex-Newfield High athlete, middleweights; Billy Plant, willing welterweight mixer, and Weldon Cleas, 118-pounder from Levittown.

Menna, who was a crowd pleaser as a pro, particu-

Article/picture in *New York Daily News*.

Eight
Meeting Bob Dylan...Almost

Gail Higgins, whom I met at Nassau Community College and became good friends with, was smart and had a great smile, a great laugh, and a wonderful family. She and her friend Diane were able to get tickets for any concert or show at the Fillmore East, Madison Square Garden, the Felt Forum, or the Palladium. She called me one Sunday morning.

"I have two tickets for the tribute concert for Woody Guthrie at Carnegie Hall. Do you want them?"

"Why don't you want to go?"

"I can't go. I have to work."

After we decided how I'd pick up the tickets, I called Steve and asked him if he also wanted to go. He did.

Tickets for this concert were impossible to get for a couple of reasons. First, because it was a tribute concert for Woody Guthrie with several big names performing – Joan Baez, Pete Seeger, Woody's son Arlo, Tom Paxton, Jack Elliott, Odetta, Richie Havens, Country Joe McDonald, Earl Robinson – and secondly, because there was a rumor that Bob Dylan might be there. Dylan hadn't been seen in over a year and a half since he had been injured in a motorcycle accident in Woodstock, N.Y.

On our way there, we couldn't stop talking about how cool it would be to see Dylan. As it turned out, besides seeing him perform, we tried to meet him in person.

Our seats were in the tenth row.

The concert had an unusual format. Instead of each performer coming out individually to perform, they all walked out together, including Dylan, and sat on chairs arranged across the stage. The performers only stood up when they sang or when they provided backup for each other.

Dylan was wearing a grey suit, a blue shirt, and black suede boots, and had a beard and moustache. He looked so cool. When he got up to sing, his backup band, The Band, joined him.

After everyone sang, there was an intermission. Steve and I went outside and got coffee. We decided to stand by the stage door to see if we'd see any of the performers.

While we were standing there, we got an idea. Maybe we could sneak in by following one of the performers, pretending to be with them, and maybe meet Dylan. We agreed that this wasn't something either of us had ever done before, but it might be fun to try. What did we have to lose?

A few minutes later, we had our chance. Jack Elliott walked right by us, smiled, and walked in. We followed him, about five feet behind. There was a desk on the right with a security guard, who greeted Jack as he walked in. Jack hadn't noticed that we were right behind him. So, as we walked by the guard, we gave him a nod and continued following Jack.

Just when I thought we had gotten past the guard, he stopped us and asked, "Where are you guys going?"

Steve told him, “We’re with Jack,” and continued walking.

He didn’t fall for that and told us to wait. He called, “Mr. Elliott, would you please come back here.”

Jack returned, walking right by us, and said, “What’s up?”

The guard pointed at us and asked him if he knew us.

We were trying to look like we belonged and said, “How’s it going?” We were hoping that maybe he’d think we were with one of the other performers.

He said, “I don’t know these guys,” and walked away. The guard shook his head, not looking surprised or angry, and told us, “Get out.” Luckily, we were able to return to our seats for the rest of the show.

The second half of the concert was better than the first half. The audience was really into the concert, with people dancing and joining in to sing.

Dylan was electric. All the way home we couldn’t stop talking about how we almost met him and what we would have said to him if we had.

Nine
Manpower and Models

Sometimes when Hofstra was closed for holidays, Steve and I would try to make some money by doing temporary work at a place called Manpower. It was a hiring agency, located in Hempstead, Long Island, that specialized in short-term job placement. We were only looking to work for a day or two and make some quick money, but this one time it turned out to be much more than another job.

You needed to get there early to get any work, which we did. The dispatcher told us that B. Altman and Company, an upscale department store located on the Miracle Mile in Manhasset, Long Island, needed a couple of dish-washers. We took the job and drove over there to meet the kitchen manager. He told us what we were going to do and brought us over to the kitchen. There he gave us a couple of aprons and showed us how to load this large industrial dishwasher. We stayed busy since their cafeteria was known for their good food. All day long we loaded dishes and glasses onto large trays and ran them through it. After the trays came out, we'd stack them for the waiters and waitresses.

It wasn't too exciting, but it was a job and we got to work together. At the end of the day, the kitchen manager asked us, "Would you guys like to work as busboys next week at a fashion show we're having for our top customers?" Since the show was at night, it wouldn't interfere with school, so we told him we would.

The following week, we arrived wearing black jeans and white shirts, like we were told to wear. He wanted us to help set up tables, chairs, and the presentation area. But since the receptionist wasn't there when people started arriving, the manager asked us if we could work the door. He was adamant and said, "No one is allowed to go in unless they're on the list that I'm giving you."

As we were looking at the list a woman walked by us and tried to enter. We stopped her and asked, "What's your name?" She looked annoyed. She told us her name, but it wasn't on the list so we told her she couldn't enter. She said, "I'm the person who put this show together, and I'm the models' chaperone." She was annoyed and briskly walked into the large room. I heard her say, under her breath, "Idiots."

In a little while the receptionist arrived, so we returned to setting up tables. This run-in with the woman turned out to be ironic because the next night we were in a similar situation.

The show started, and while I was staying busy clearing tables I noticed Steve talking to a couple of the models. Since that seemed like more fun, I got rid of my tray of glasses and joined them. After a few minutes, the woman who we had had the run-in with walked over to us and told the models that they should be mingling with the guests, not with the help, and in a stern voice said to us, "You're supposed to be working, busing the tables, not talking to the models. Do your job." What a bitch.

After the show, while we were cleaning up, the models came over to us. They said they were doing another fashion show at another B. Altman store in White Plains the following night, and they asked us if we'd like to be their dates. They were dolls, so of course we said yes.

Although they were supposed to meet us at the front door the next night, when we arrived, they weren't there.

Steve said, "Maybe they're busy getting ready for the show and put our names on the guest list."

We went over to the receptionist and gave him our names. He looked the list over a couple of times and told us our names weren't on it.

I said, "We're meeting a couple of the models, and if we could go in and find them, they could vouch for us," but the receptionist said, "No one's allowed to go in unless they're on the list." It sounded familiar since we had said the same thing the night before. He said, "Please step aside."

While we were standing there trying to figure out what to do, the woman who had yelled at us the previous night came over. She asked the receptionist, "Why are they standing here? Is there a problem?"

"They claim that they're supposed to meet a couple of the models, but they're not on the list."

She looked at us, smiled, and said hello. She asked us, "What's going on?"

We told her that after the fashion show the previous night, the girls had invited us to be their dates at this show. To our complete surprise, she turned to the receptionist and said, "There must be some mistake. They definitely should be on the list." She went on to tell him, "These gentlemen are famous actors. I saw them perform last night."

We were shocked! As she escorted us into the show, we thanked her, big time.

After the show, we decided to push our luck and asked the girls if they could go back to the city with us and hang out.

They said, "It's up to our chaperone since we're supposed to go back with her and the other girls." Outside was a limo waiting for them.

We walked over to the chaperone with them, and I asked her, "Can we take girls back to the city?"

Again she surprised us and said, "Okay, but you have to promise to get them back to their hotel no later than eleven p.m." They were staying at the Barbizon, a famous hotel for women only. It was located on 63rd Street and Lexington Avenue, and was known for the strict policy of an 11 p.m. curfew.

We promised her we would. We went to One-Fifth, a cool, trendy restaurant on lower 5th Avenue. We had a couple of drinks and some snacks since the girls hadn't eaten yet. They were interesting and told us about the shows they had just got back from in Milan and Paris. We told them that we went to Hofstra University and were art majors.

We went out with them a few times, but the reality was that we were a couple of college guys, and they were beautiful models traveling around the world. We didn't have a whole lot in common besides our physical attraction, which was more than fine.

Ten
Driving a Taxi in New York City

During our junior year at Hofstra University, Steve and I decided to get taxi licenses and make some money driving cabs in New York City.

Getting a taxi license was easy. You had to have a driver's license and a birth certificate, and you had to pass a written test given by the Taxi and Limousine Commission. The test was twenty questions that required you to know the addresses of various tourist places in the city, e.g., the Empire State Building, Central Park, the Metropolitan Museum of Art, Wall Street, Yankee Stadium, and Madison Square Garden.

We took the test at their office, and it was graded while we waited. We both passed. Once we had our licenses, we had to find a taxi garage that needed drivers.

We were told that we'd have a better chance of finding a garage that needed a driver by going to different ones individually. Most garages that I went to looked alike, and most of the garages were in Queens.

They were usually dark, with fluorescent lights that gave off an icy white light. Some had windows that were so dirty light couldn't enter, and everything looked greasy. Some garages had one or two cars that were being worked on.

When I asked the dispatcher at the first garage if he needed a driver, in a low voice he said, "Do you see any cabs?"

I looked around and didn't.

"We don't make money with cabs sitting around. I don't need nobody." Then he said, "There's another garage a few blocks away that's looking for a driver."

The next garage did need a driver and told me to come back the next week. Steve also got a job at a garage near the one where I did, so every Friday we'd drive in together after classes were over.

The shifts were five a.m. to four p.m. or five p.m. to four a.m. They weren't strict with the time you brought your car in as long as you made money. Sometimes after work we'd crash at the apartment of our friend Richie (who owned Instant Pants) and his girlfriend Darian, which was near the garages. Later on, I came to realize driving the night shift was a lot different than the day shift.

Going to work was the same routine. I'd report to the dispatcher, who would tell me the number of the cab I was driving, then give me the keys and a trip sheet. It was an 11" x 14" piece of brown paper with columns where you would write where you picked someone up and the time, where you dropped them off and the time, and the fare.

Most cabs didn't have radios, so I usually brought my portable cassette player with several tapes. Once I crossed over the 59th Street Bridge, I always started by driving downtown. I'd drive down the middle lane so that I could pick someone up on either side of the street.

I always thought of my cab as my traveling office. When I first started driving, I was always anxious. Partly because I didn't know how to get around and partly because I had to deal with so many different people. Some were drunk or high, and sometimes they would fall asleep, which was a weird thing to have to deal with. Sometimes when I woke them up, they didn't know where they were and became aggressive, throwing punches. Some people didn't want to get out of the cab but wanted to be left alone to sleep.

Once I got some experience, driving was a lot more fun and less stressful. I learned how to deal with these different types of people. But it was always something. Some customers complained that I was going too fast or too slow. If I got stuck in traffic, I would be accused of doing it on purpose. They'd say, "I know what you're doing. You're trying to run the meter up to charge me more, but this additional money will come out of your tip." Swell.

Some people got annoyed if I didn't know how to get them where they wanted to go. They assumed cabbies knew every street. Above 14th Street it was fairly easy to get around because the streets are basically a grid of avenues and streets, e.g., 89th Street and 2nd Avenue or 39th and 5th. But below Houston Street, the streets get a little tricky because most of them have names, e.g., Greene Street, Crosby Street, Carmine Street, and Cornelia Street. Too bad I didn't have GPS then.

CBGB & Max's Kansas City

Some nights it was so slow it seemed that no one wanted a cab. When that happened, I'd sometimes take a break and meet my friends at CBGB or Max's. Hilly, who owned CBGB and worked the door, knew me and my friends (Gail, Denise, Janis, Steve, Abbi

Jane, and Johnny). We went there often and never had a problem getting in. I'd hang out with them and have a beer. Sometimes, instead of leaving and continuing driving, I'd let them all pack into my cab – of course, I wouldn't turn the meter on – and we'd go to Max's. We'd go upstairs to listen to whomever was playing. After a while I'd leave and return to driving. Those nights I didn't make much money, but I had fun.

Drive Like a Bucking Bronco

One night I picked up a businessman in midtown. After getting in and telling me where he wanted to go, he said, "I'm from Texas and I'd like you to drive like you're a bucking bronco." A what? This was a first. So, all the way to his hotel, I would floor the car as soon as the light turned green, going as fast as I could, and at red lights I would jam on my brakes. This guy was bouncing around, sliding all over the back seat. It was a riot. When we got to his hotel, he was laughing. He said thanks and gave me a large tip.

Eleven
A Dangerous Saturday Night

After I moved into the city, I started working for another taxi garage. One dreary Saturday afternoon while I was sitting in my loft watching a light rain fall, I was thinking about being broke again. So I decided to go to the taxi garage and see if they had a car available. I took the subways uptown and walked to the garage. I couldn't believe what a dreary, depressing day it was.

When I got there, I was in luck. The dispatcher told me that he had a couple of cabs that weren't being used, and he was happy to accommodate me. Usually, when it rained I did well and didn't have to work too late.

As soon as I dropped one passenger off, another one would get in. Everyone was in a hurry and impatient. Although I was busy, this night felt a little strange. The rain finally stopped at ten p.m. Sometimes after it rained, the lights from the stores or traffic lights reflected off the streets and looked beautiful, but tonight they looked eerily colorful.

After midnight I was thinking about bringing my car in. I had had a busy night, but I got a little greedy and figured I'd pick up one more fare. I was on the Lower East Side. The only places open were bars and a few delis. The streets were dark and desolate.

While I was stopped at a light, two guys jumped into my cab.

"Where do you want to go?" I asked. I didn't like the looks of them and was hoping for a short trip.

"Long Island City in Queens," said the older one as he slammed the door.

"Gonna meet a friend there," said the other one. They both chuckled.

I had no idea what they thought was funny, which added to my feeling of nervousness. They were probably in their twenties, and they were very jittery. I told them I didn't know how to get there, although I did, hoping that they'd get out.

"Don't worry. We'll tell you."

So I headed up First Avenue where, at this time of night, if you're lucky you could make every light to the 59th Street Bridge that took you into Queens. I tried to engage them in conversation, but they didn't seem to want to talk to me, so I turned on my cassette player and tried to relax a little, which wasn't easy. Whenever I looked in my rear-view mirror, they were whispering to each other as if they were making a plan. I kept thinking that I should have locked the doors and brought my taxi in earlier. I didn't have a good feeling about these guys.

After going over the bridge they started giving me directions. I kept one eye on the streets and one eye on them. One guy did all the talking. The other guy, who seemed to have developed a twitch, kept looking around nervously. The area they directed me to was an industrial area that was probably busy during the day, but it was deserted now.

After making several turns, they said, "We're almost there."

As I made another turn, I really got worried when I saw a street sign, "Dead End." My heart started beating faster. As I made the turn they said, "Our friend is going to meet us at the end of the street."

As we got close to the end of the street, I didn't see anyone, so I decided I had to make my move. I jammed on my brakes and said, "This is as far as I go."

They looked surprised and asked, "What's the fare?" Instead of putting the money in the slot in the Plexiglas divider that separated me from them, they got out. One guy got out on my side, and the other guy got out on the other side. As soon as they got out, I locked the doors. The guy on my side asked me to roll down my window so he could pay me. But out of the corner of my right eye, I saw the other guy trying to open the door. He had a knife. I immediately put the cab in reverse, driving backwards all the way up to the intersection as fast as I could. At the corner I threw my car in drive and fishtailing out of there. My heart was beating so fast that I thought it was going to jump out of my chest.

I drove straight to the garage. I was still shaking when I told the night dispatcher what happened. After giving him the money for the night and my trip sheet, he said, "Don't worry, it happens all the time. You wouldn't have had to pay their fare." As I was talking to the dispatcher, the guy who gassed up the cars and wiped the insides down walked over to me and handed me a knife that he said was on the back seat. I figured it must have fallen out of the other guy's pocket. I told him to keep it.

What a night.

TAXICAB DRIVER'S LICENSE
EXPIRES: MAY 31, 1977

WELDON R.
CLEARS

Hack Number

2 8 6 8 5 9

See Other Side For Any Restrictions

CORRECTIVE LENSES

NEW YORK CITY TAXI and LIMOUSINE COMMISSION
87 BEAVER STREET, N.Y., N.Y. 10005 - MOSES L. KOVE Chairman

50M-213076(75)

04778

NEW YORK CITY TAXI and LIMOUSINE COMMISSION
87 BEAVER STREET, NEW YORK, NY, 10005
TAXICAB DRIVER'S LICENSE

EXPIRES MAY 31, 1975

WELDON R.
CLEARS

2 5 5 1 3 6

RESTRICTIONS

TLC-TDL-50M-M312049 (73)

MICHAEL J. LAZAR, Chairman

Twelve
College and the Draft

While I was experiencing all these adventures and also attending classes, the war in Vietnam continued. So did the need for more troops. It seemed that every week there were protests and demonstrations about something. The war, women's rights, or civil rights. One day there might be a demonstration at school, or maybe Alan Ginsberg and his boyfriend would be on campus talking about gay rights or protesting the Vietnam war. He coined the phrase "Flower Power."

In 1969, there was a demonstration in Washington, D.C. Thousands of antiwar protesters marched against the war in Vietnam. It was called the Moratorium March. Everyone went, including Steve, a couple of our friends, and me. It was a great show of solidarity.

As we were walking around the White House, the National Guard decided to break us up and fired tear gas at us. Everyone started running. It was pandemonium. The tear gas burned everyone's eyes; we could hardly see. Some people were trampled. After running a couple of blocks, we found someone who had water that we used to rinse our eyes. After doing that, we rejoined the march.

Later we met some friends and hung out in the President's Park. At night we joined a huge march up Pennsylvania Avenue to the White House. After the march we returned to the park and slept there. The next day we drove home, feeling great that we went.

As the need for more troops in Vietnam continued to escalate, the government kept changing the requirements for a student deferment. My status was in jeopardy every time they did this. In the beginning, just going to college was enough. But the new qualification was that you had to be in the top ten per cent of your class. This didn't bode well for me since I had a solid C average. That summer I took four courses and got A's in all of them, which put me in the top ten per cent group.

As the intensity of the war continued, the need for even more troops grew. The government again changed the requirements for a student deferment and decided to have a lottery. So, on December 1, 1969, the Selective Service of the United States conducted a lottery for men born between 1944 and 1950. The lottery was based upon your birthdate. Depending on when you were born you would be assigned a number that would indicate if you'd be drafted when you graduated or stopped attending college.

The night they held the draft lottery, Steve and I were working in his parents' basement filling some orders for belts. In the background we had the radio on to hear our fates. Someone at school said, "Anyone whose birthdate number was below 125 would probably be drafted once their current classification ended." I couldn't believe it when they announced that my number was 29, Steve's was 195. Now I knew that as soon as I graduated, I would be drafted.

The next morning at school, I asked some of the other guys who had low numbers what they were going to do. Some of my friends were in ROTC, the Reserve Officers Training Corps, which basically paid for college in exchange for your agreement to serve in the military. Several guys said they were moving to Canada when they graduated, and others claimed they were going to act gay because the military didn't permit homosexuals. One of the most amazing stories I heard was about a guy who said that after graduating he was going to blind himself in one eye by looking at the flame of a metal welders' torch. He felt that it was better than being killed in Vietnam. Just imagine making that decision.

Some guys said they were going to get jobs that had a union that automatically gave them a deferment. A few guys said that they were going to find a doctor who was sympathetic to those that didn't want to serve and would write a letter saying that they were unfit for military service so they would receive a 4F classification.

I didn't know what I was going to do, but I definitely knew I had to decide soon since I was graduating in six months.

The months flew by.

One May Day five months later, when I was walking over the overpass at Hofstra from the parking lot to the main campus, I saw several of my friends sitting around talking. I asked them why they weren't going to class.

They said, "School's closed. There's no more classes."

"Because of all the demonstrations and what occurred at Kent State University, where four students had been killed while demonstrating, all colleges are closing."

Depending on your grades, you could ask your professor for a P pass, or if you had an F and wanted to bring your grade up, you could take a final.

I opted for a P. Except my Art History professor wouldn't agree to give me a P. She wanted me to take the final since I was doing well, and with a good grade on the final, I could ace the course.

I told her, "I don't care about getting an A," but she insisted that I read a book. She wanted me to read a book about the Chicago School of Design. Then she wanted me to meet her at her apartment and give her an oral report in a week.

To my surprise the book was good. The Chicago School of Design was a group of architects and engineers in the late 19th century who were the first to promote a new technology and design, using steel-frame construction in commercial buildings.

A week later I gave her my oral report, and I got an A.

News reporters like Walter Cronkite were saying that the war in Vietnam was a losing proposition with casualties in the tens of thousands. But President Nixon kept expanding the war. Things were getting worse.

As expected, a couple of weeks later I received a letter from my draft board stating that on Friday, August 28, at six a.m. I was scheduled to report for my second physical exam at Fort Hamilton, and I should expect to be inducted. The letter said to bring some extra clothes and a toothbrush, and to notify my family that I probably wouldn't be back…for a while.

This was not good news.

My options seemed limited. I wasn't going to move to Canada, I wasn't going to act gay, I definitely wasn't going to blind myself, nor did I know of any union I could join. The only doctor I knew was our family doctor who I never talked to, so I didn't have any idea how he felt about the war in Vietnam.

After asking around, someone told me about a chiropractor that was sympathetic to guys trying to get out of the draft. I made an appointment with him right away. I wasn't sure if I should ask for a letter right away or pretend that I had a bad back and build up a case. I decided on the latter.

I saw him twice a week for three weeks, claiming that my lower back was hurting and that I might have pulled it while I was working at Jones Beach cleaning the pool. One day when he was working on me, I told him, "I just received a letter from my draft board scheduling me for a physical and saying that if I pass, I'll probably be drafted." I asked him if he'd write a letter to my draft board explaining to them that my back was so bad I wasn't fit to serve.

He said he'd be glad to.

The next morning, I drove to my draft board with the letter. I was feeling good. I thought I was so smart and that the money I spent seeing him was money well spent.

When I arrived at my draft board in Freeport, L.I., I gave the letter to a woman at the front desk, telling her it was a letter from my doctor saying that I had a bad back and wasn't healthy enough to serve. I was hoping that she'd cancel my physical on the spot.

She smiled, read the letter, and handed it to another woman who also read it. She also smiled and then said, "Honey, the AMA (American Medical Association) doesn't accept nor recognize the opinion of chiropractors when it pertained to a draftee's health, and neither does the US Army."

I was shocked and couldn't say anything.

She smiled and gave me back my letter and told me, "Don't forget to show up."

I wasn't sure what I was going to do.

Losing Weight

Somewhere in the back of my mind I remembered someone saying that if you were underweight, whatever that weight was, it would be enough to automatically fail you. Maybe that's why the guy at my first physical told me to bulk up.

So, the summer of 1970, starting the third week of June, I began to lose weight. Knowing that I only had two months to do this made it seem impossible. At the time I weighed 168 pounds. I had gained some weight since I stopped boxing and was the heaviest I had ever been. The challenge was that I didn't know how to diet, nor did I know how much weight I'd have to lose to be considered underweight. I decided that since I weighed 118 pounds at my first physical, I'd choose that as my target.

Losing fifty pounds would normally be hard, but since I was sharing a summer house with four other guys who worked at Jones Beach, it was even harder. Potato chips, pretzels, pizza, and beer were always around. Also, every night we would hang out at the local bars drinking, which made it even more difficult.

The first two weeks I lost five pounds by cutting out one meal a day – breakfast. Then I started taking amphetamines and cutting out lunch. I got down twenty pounds, but I had to stop taking the pills because they made me feel too jittery.

I wasn't sure what to do next. I stopped drinking beer and eating junk food like ice cream, french fries, and potato chips. Finally, I only ate one meal a day, which helped but not much. I definitely had to do something more drastic since the date for my physical was getting closer, so I decided to sweat off the pounds.

Every day after work, I'd put on several layers of clothes – pajamas, a rubber sweat suit, sweatshirt, and sweatpants. I'd get into my car, a Rambler, turn the heat all the way up, and drive around Long Island for hours, sweating and listening to music. I was a man on a mission.

I continued to do this every day. When August arrived, knowing I only had a few weeks left, I decided to cut out eating all together. When I was hungry or thirsty, I'd suck on an ice cube. By August 27th I had reached my goal, losing fifty pounds. My waist went from thirty-two inches to twenty-six inches.

The night before my physical I had dinner with my parents, though of course I didn't eat. I told them, "I might not return after my physical." I kissed them and said good-bye.

I don't think I slept at all that night. Finally, the day I had been waiting for arrived. I got dressed and drove to my draft board in the dark, not knowing my fate. Just in case I didn't fail my physical, I brought a small gym bag with some clothes and a toothbrush, like they suggested.

I pulled into the parking lot of the draft board and saw a yellow school bus waiting. When I got on the bus, I saw that it was half full. Everyone looked sleepy and glum, just like I was feeling.

Once we got to Fort Hamilton, they separated us into different groups. While we were on line they gave everyone a blue-covered book like the kind we used in high school to take tests. They used it to record the scores of your written test, blood pressure, vision, hearing, eye exam, weight, height, and any comments.

The physical was extensive and lasted all day. There must have been several hundred guys taking their physicals. At noon they gave us lunch, which of course I didn't have. My book had all sorts of scores and comments in it.

At the last desk, a soldier looked over the information in my book, gave me a look, and then wrote across the front of my book,

"Underweight." He told me, "You're underweight and failed your physical. You'll be receiving a 4F classification."

I almost jumped for joy. All I could think about was that I wasn't going to Vietnam.

The first thing I did was call my mom. The second thing I did was call my friend Pam Graham. She was cute, smart, and had a good sense of humor. We had made a pact that if I failed my physical, we would drive across the United States to California.

After the bus returned me and the other guys who failed their physicals to Freeport, I got into my car, this time without the heater on and with all the windows rolled down. I drove to the nearest Wendy's, where I had a double cheeseburger, large fries, and a vanilla shake. I'll never forget how good it tasted.

Demonstrating at Hofstra University, 1969.
Steve is in the middle, and I'm on the right.

Thirteen
Trip to California

1970

After I called Pam and told her the good news, we agreed to leave in two weeks. She wanted to go to California to visit her mom. I wanted to go to Southern California, preferably Newport Beach, where some friends I knew from high school lived. I planned on getting an apartment and a job and living there for a while.

Pam had an Opel Kadett, made by GM, with an eight-track tape player and several tapes: Joni Mitchell, Joan Baez, Linda Ronstadt, Janis Joplin, and the Supremes. I also had several eight-track tapes, since one of my cars had an eight-track tape player. I added to her collection of tapes: Led Zeppelin, the Rolling Stones, Traffic, 10 Years After, the Beatles, Santana, and Crosby, Stills and Nash.

At the same time we were planning our trip, two of my high school friends, Larry Vichnis and Tom Conway, were also planning a trip to California. One night while we were at happy hour, we decided that since we were leaving the same day and were going to visit the same friends, we would coordinate our trips and visit our friends at the same time.

Tom and Larry got an Austin Healy from a company called AACON. AACON hired drivers to drive cars for people who were moving but didn't have time or the desire to drive their cars to where they were moving. Tom and Larry lucked out and got a driving assignment to drive a car to Southern California.

Our first stop was Canton, Ohio, where our friend Pat was going to Walsh College. After visiting and partying for a couple of days, we drove north and visited our friend Joel, who was a student teacher at the College of Kalamazoo in Michigan, and we stayed there for a couple of days.

Our next stop was St. Louis to visit our friend Joe. He worked at the University of Missouri in the Provost's office and was able to reserve the university's Harry S. Truman suite. It was used for dignitaries, visitors, and alumni, and this time for us. The suite was beautiful. It was large, with wood paneling. We stayed for a couple of days visiting some of the sites, including the Anheuser-Busch Brewery, of course, and the Gateway Arch. At night we would meet Joe for dinner and go to a couple of the local bars. Next stop was Las Vegas.

Traveling across the United States was great. Each state was so different and beautiful in its own way. Pam and I agreed that we were having more fun than we thought we would. The trip was exhilarating.

Las Vegas

Pam and I arrived in Las Vegas late in the afternoon. The sun was setting, and the lights on the huge neon marquees were as bright as the lights on Broadway. We were so excited to be there.

As we were driving down the Strip looking for a place to stay, we saw a marquee at one of the hotels announcing that the

Supremes were performing there. Pam said, “The Supremes are my favorite group. I would love to see them.” At that moment I decided that I’d surprise her and try to get tickets for their show.

After we checked into a motel, Pam took a nap. I went out to pick up some soda and snacks, and also go to the box office at the hotel where the Supremes were appearing to try to get tickets. I was really looking forward to surprising her.

When I got to the box office, I asked, “Can I get two tickets for tonight’s show?”

“No problem.”

I couldn’t believe how lucky I was to score two tickets. Unfortunately, later I realized that I should have been specific and asked for tickets for the Supremes’ show.

After I returned to the motel, we showered, changed, and went to dinner. It was a warm, beautiful night. We found a place to eat right on the Strip. We couldn’t stop talking about how cool it was to be in Las Vegas. The lights, the hotels, the people, the marquees – just like we pictured it. After dinner we strolled along the Strip. I was filled with excitement knowing that the best was yet to come… At least that’s what I thought.

As we walked along, I gently guided Pam towards the hotel where the show was. As we got close, she saw the marquee and said, “I wish we could see them.”

“We are.” I told her that while she was napping, I got tickets. She screamed and gave me a hug.

We entered the hotel and made our way over to the concert venue. I felt great, and she looked the happiest I ever saw her. The place was filling up as we were brought over to a small table where we ordered a couple of drinks and got ready for what was sure to be a super show and a night to remember.

The lights dimmed, a band began to play, and out walked… Jimmy Durante. Jimmy Durante was a well-known classic vaudeville comedian, a class act. I'd seen him on Ed Sullivan.

I thought it was strange that he was the opening act, so I called over the waitress and asked her, "Is he the opening act for the Supremes?"

She said, "No, he's the show's headliner."

I was shocked. "What about the Supremes?"

She said, "I'm sorry. The Supremes were here the week before, but the marquee hasn't yet been updated with this show." The waitress apologized again for the confusion and said that we weren't the only people who were expecting to see the Supremes.

I couldn't believe it, and neither could Pam. The waitress was nice and offered to give us a second round of drinks on the house. I apologized to Pam for the mix-up and explained to her what I had done or not done. I felt so bad. Pam, being the good sport she was, said, "That's ok, we'll still have fun." I wanted to leave and sulk about my stupidity, but we stayed.

She was right. The show turned out to be really good, and we had some good laughs. I still couldn't believe I didn't ask the guy in the box office who was appearing that night and that I didn't even look at the tickets.

Pam and I met Larry and Tom the next day and stayed in Vegas for a couple of days visiting the hotels, doing a little gambling, and seeing the Hoover Dam. Before leaving we told them that we'd meet them in Newport Beach at our friend John's house and then go directly to San Francisco, where Pam's mother lived.

After arriving in Newport Beach, Tom and Larry joined us, and we all drove up to San Francisco. Once we got there, we met Pam's mother and her boyfriend, Larry. They were very friendly, and when they heard that we didn't have a place to stay, they said we could stay there for a couple of days.

The next morning we did some tourist stuff, visiting Haight-Ashbury, the Golden Gate Bridge, and Sausalito. In the afternoon we went back to the house and sat by their pool drinking beer we had picked up while Larry, Pam's mother's boyfriend, made delicious tacos.

By coincidence, while we were there, one of Pam's brothers, Tim, was also visiting his mom but staying at a friend's apartment. He came by the next day and hung out with us by the pool.

Tim said that he was leaving the next day to go back to Wantagh, Long Island, where he lived. He said, "I'm headed south, down Route 1 to Las Vegas before heading home." Tom, Larry, and I asked him if we could get a lift since Newport Beach was south, so he wouldn't have to go too much out of his way to drop us off.

He said, "Sure, driving down the coast with you guys will be fun."

This was perfect since we didn't have any other way to get back to Newport Beach. The next day Tim came by to spend some quality time with his mom and Pam. After a late lunch he decided it was time to leave. We thanked Pam's mom and Larry for their hospitality.

I was a little sad saying good-bye to Pam. I told her how much fun I had with her and what a great trip it was and that I'd miss her. Then we piled into the back of Tim's VW van and headed south.

San Luis Obispo

Since we left a little later than we had expected, when we got to San Luis Obispo, the halfway point between San Francisco and Newport Beach, Tim decided to stop for the night. He parked at the end of a dead-end street right by the beach. Since there wasn't enough room for all of us to sleep in the van, Tom, Larry, and I grabbed our sleeping bags to sleep on the beach. Although it's hard to believe, we didn't notice that we walked over railroad tracks to get to a shack we had decided to sleep behind so no one would see us. This shack was about ten feet from the tracks.

At two in the morning I woke up because the beach had begun to vibrate. At first I thought I was dreaming, but I wasn't. The ground was shaking, so I figured that maybe it was an earthquake. In the distance I heard a loud rumbling sound. At this point, Larry also woke up and asked me what was happening. I told him I didn't know, but as we looked around, we saw a light that was getting larger coming towards us, and the rumbling sound got louder. When it was about two hundred yards away, we realized that it was a train with several cars attached and that we were next to the tracks. As it went by, the sound was deafening. What a way to wake up. To our surprise Tom never woke up.

The next morning, we got back in the van, and Tim drove us to our friend's house. Tim then continued on his way.

Fourteen
Newport Beach

When we arrived at our friend's house, Larry and Tom were told that John's roommate had changed his mind and didn't want them to stay there, which they were planning on doing.

John said, "You can probably get a small apartment at the Newport Beach Hotel, just a few blocks away." So we decided to check it out.

The hotel was right on the beach, and to our surprise, it had a small studio apartment for rent that was seventy-five dollars a month. The studio would have been small for one person. For three guys it was ridiculous, but we were determined to make it work.

Living in Newport Beach was a trip. The room was on the second floor. It had a bed and an area that we were told was the kitchen. The "kitchen" had a hot plate, a sink, a very small refrigerator, and cabinets where we could store pots, pans, plates and glasses, all stuff we didn't have. The bathroom had a window, a sink, and a toilet. The hotel had showers on each floor, but they were outside at the end of the hall. It wasn't uncommon to see men and women walking around with just a towel wrapped around them; we soon became three of those people. At the other end of the hall, next to the stairs was a large window that looked out onto the beach.

Our apartment wasn't much, but we were happy to have a place to stay, especially one right on the beach. After moving in, I suggested that we pool our money and come up with some kind of budget. They said, "We don't have any money. We spent it all on the trip." Swell. I had some money and realized if we were going to live together, I'd have to share it. Tom said, "It seems that your money is our money." He was right.

There was only one bed, so we figured we'd take turns sleeping in it. Tom was lucky because after sleeping on the floor, Larry and I told him he could have the bed since we didn't mind sleeping on the floor. Every night we'd roll our sleeping bags out, and in the morning we'd roll them up.

The day after moving in, the three of us went shopping. We got plates, glasses, a pot, a pan, and some food.

I was the cook by default since they didn't know how to cook. I didn't mind it since my mom taught me some basic things when I was growing up. I'd make breakfast and dinner; we usually didn't eat lunch.

To make this arrangement fair, Tom and Larry's responsibilities were to clean up. Since we only had a hot plate and limited funds, I didn't cook anything fancy like meat. Pasta with tomato sauce, oatmeal, eggs, and mashed potatoes were our main meals. These dishes were easy to make and cheap; we never missed a meal. We also discovered a wine called "Red Mountain" that only cost five dollars a gallon and soon became our drink of choice.

Since we had all worked at Jones Beach that summer, we were entitled to collect unemployment. It required that we had to look for a job. We looked in the newspaper but never could find one. After a few weeks, Tom and I started receiving our unemployment checks, which helped since my funds were getting low. Although Larry also filed for unemployment, he never received any checks, which was strange.

Besides going shopping and to the unemployment office, we also went to the library every couple of weeks.

Since I was the first one to wake up, I'd make coffee, pour myself a cup, walk outside to the end of the hall, and look out the large window to check out the beach and the waves. I loved starting my day this way.

Newport Beach was beautiful, and in spite of our living conditions, we were happy to live there. Some days when we weren't busy, we'd take a blanket and sit on the beach reading our books. The beach was usually empty. There'd be some people walking their dogs, but that was it. It was usually sunny and in the mid-sixties. Some days were even warmer.

One morning as I was walking down the hall, I heard a lot of noise outside. When I got to the window, I saw hundreds of people on the beach and in the street. I actually thought that they were filming a Gidget movie.

The temperature must have been in the 80s, and the beach was crowded with people in bathing suits watching the surfers. I leaned out the window and asked a girl what was going on. She said that the Santa Ana winds had arrived. We found out later that the Santa Ana winds are strong, extremely dry, warm winds that come from inland and affect coastal Southern California, usually in the fall.

I went back to the room and woke the guys, telling them what was going on. Right after breakfast we put on our bathing suits and went to the beach to join everyone else. What a surprise it was to go unexpectedly from one day of sixty degrees with just a few people on the beach to eighty-five degrees and see the beach crowded.

Another morning I was awakened by the sound of our few dishes and glasses rattling and then falling out of our kitchen cabinets. Our whole apartment was shaking. I wasn't sure what was happening but guessed it was an earthquake. I immediately got up and walked down the hall to see if there was a tsunami. There wasn't, so I returned to our room. By then Larry and Tom were also awake. We waited to see if anything else was going to happen, but after several minutes the shaking stopped, and they went back to sleep. Later that day we heard that it was in fact an earthquake and a fairly big one with over sixty people dying and doing damage into the hundreds of millions. It became known as the 1971 San Fernando earthquake.

Meeting Our Next-door Neighbor

Our first meeting with our next-door neighbor at the hotel was an unusual one.

It was another beautiful day, and we had just returned from the beach. Suddenly there was a knock at our door. Since we had already paid the rent, we knew it wasn't the hotel manager and since no one ever visited us, we had no idea who it could be. I got up and opened the door.

Standing there was this guy in shorts and a wrinkled tee shirt with long hair. He said, "Hi, I'm your next-door neighbor. I'm Bones. Can I use your bathroom?"

I looked at Larry and Tom and let Bones in. He said hi to them and went into our bathroom. We looked at each and shook our heads.

Larry said in a low whisper, "What's that all about?" A few minutes later Tom looked out the window which was next to his bed, where you could see the bathroom window, and said, "Bones is climbing out the window onto the fire escape." As Bones walked by, he saw us and said, "Thanks." How strange.

About an hour later, there was another knock on the door. I opened the door, and it was Bones again with another guy, who he said was one of his roommates. I invited them in, and we introduced ourselves. Since we didn't have any chairs, we all sat on the floor.

Bones then told us why he had to climb through our bathroom window. "Sometimes I forget the key to my apartment, which is right next door, so instead of bothering the hotel manager for my key, I climb through your bathroom window and take the fire escape to my apartment."

We all agreed that made sense. Tom told him, "We're from New York and just arrived. We're unemployed and just hanging out in Newport for a few months."

His roommate said that they were also unemployed and hanging out. "Once we get some money, we're going to rent a nicer place."

From the way they looked and since they didn't work, I didn't know how that was going to happen. They also smelled like they didn't know that there were showers at the end of the hall.

After a while they got up. Bones thanked us again, and they left. We rarely saw them after that, and he never asked to use our bathroom again.

Living in that hotel was certainly different.

Our social life was ok considering our limited social and financial situation. Sometimes our friend Bob, who we went to high school with, and Olga, his wife, or John would pick us up and take us to one of the many bars in the area or to a party. The girls we met were friendly and liked our New York accents and our curly hair. What accents?

The Sunshine Festival

Our first Christmas in California turned out to be another trip that we weren't planning on taking.

Christmas Day morning, Bob and Olga picked us up at our hotel to go to an outdoor concert in Laguna Canyon. The concert was called the Sunshine Festival in Laguna Canyon. People got word of a big happening – The Great Happening – The Christmas Happening of 1970, that was put together by the Brotherhood of Eternal Love, who were followers and friends of Timothy Leary, a Harvard professor who advocated using psychedelic drugs like LSD. Thousands of people showed up.

Going to a concert on Christmas Day instead of opening gifts with my family was an unusual way to spend the day.

We drove down the Coast Highway with the Pacific Ocean on our right. It was a beautiful morning. When we got to Laguna, there were hundreds of cars and hippies all over the place. Several hours later there were thousands. Bob and Olga had brought a blanket and food for all of us. We looked around and finally found a spot where we could easily see the stage. It was a little cool out but sunny.

There were rumors that Jimi Hendrix and the Grateful Dead were going to be there. They weren't. It was supposed to be a "two-day happening," but we were only staying for the day. Most people were wearing something tie-dyed. When I squinted, the crowd looked like a moving rainbow.

While we were listening to the music or the different people on stage talking about love and happiness, we saw a small plane fly over the crowd. Someone was dropping hundreds of what looked like postcards out of the plane.

People were collecting these cards and handing them out.

Bob told us that they were probably dropped by the Brotherhood of Eternal Love celebrating Timothy Leary's escape from jail the day before. Being curious, we walked over to someone who had these cards, and we each got one. On each card was glued a small tab of LSD (Orange Sunshine) with a message: "May the Great Spirit watch over you as long as the grass grows and the water flows."

As we weaved our way through the crowd, we decided to try it. Within minutes we were tripping. What a feeling. All day long we drifted in and out of reality. One minute we were listening to a band, the next minute we couldn't tell you where we were.

Late in the afternoon our friends started packing up to leave. It had been an incredible day. But there was one problem: Larry was missing. "He must have wandered off," Tom said and since we were still tripping, looking for Larry wasn't going well. With thousands of people there, trying to find Larry was futile. After looking for him for about an hour, we gave up. We hoped that he'd be all right and find his way back to the hotel, so we left. After we were dropped off at our apartment, we talked about the day and wondered what happened to Larry.

The next morning, as we had hoped, Larry showed up. He said, "I met some people and passed out in their van."

What a different Christmas.

Super Slab

Since we only had money for rent and food and a gallon of Red Mountain wine, we never had money for pot, so we rarely got high.

One night our friend John invited us to a party that was a few blocks from the hotel. It was crowded, and the music was loud with people hanging outside the house. When we got there, John met us with beers and introduced us to some of his friends. While we were talking to some girls, they asked us if we wanted to get high. Instead of a joint they offered us a pipe with hash in it. They said it was called "super slab." After a couple of hits, we agreed that it was the strongest hash we had ever had. Even though the hotel was only a few blocks away getting back to it took a little longer.

Getting Arrested

One afternoon while we were sitting around our room, we got on the subject of food and what our favorite meal was. We all agreed that it was cheeseburgers. With that in mind, we decided to walk over to the local supermarket, the El Rancho Market, and buy what I needed to make them for dinner. The thought of having cheeseburgers sounded great.

As we were walking to the supermarket, we got a stupid idea to steal the food we needed. Of course, we knew it was the wrong thing to do, but we figured that if we each took one thing, they wouldn't notice. We'd buy ketchup as if that was the reason we were there.

On our way to the supermarket, we realized Tom was wearing his army jacket, which was out of place since the temp was in the mid 60s. Larry and I were wearing baggy light sweaters. We told Tom that wearing that jacket might draw attention to him, but he didn't think so.

We decided that I would take a pack of Monterey jack cheese, Larry would take hamburger rolls, and Tom would take chopped meat and pay for the ketchup he had.

After stealing everything we needed, we walked to the checkout. Tom put the ketchup on the counter, but the cashier asked him if he would open his jacket. He pretended he didn't hear her and took out his wallet. The cashier asked again, and when he still didn't open his jacket, she called over a manager, who also asked Tom, "Would you please open your jacket," which he did.

Once he opened it, out dropped the package of chopped meat.

Since Larry and I both thought that they probably knew we had also taken something, I took out the cheese and Larry took out the buns. From the look on the manager's face it was clear that they didn't know we had taken anything. He immediately called over another manager to watch us while he called the police.

The second manager said, "I heard about you guys. You're the gang that's been robbing supermarkets in the area. I can't believe we caught you."

We told him we weren't in any gang and apologized for attempting to steal this stuff. We said we had never done this before and would never do it again, while offering to pay for everything, but he wouldn't listen to us.

Orange County Main Jail

Within minutes a cop arrived, cuffed us, threw us in the back seat of his cruiser, and brought us to the police station. Once there, he took off our cuffs, asked for ID, and booked us.

We tried to tell him what had happened, but he said, "Shut up. I don't want to hear your story." The officer then told us, "You'll be spending the night in the holding cell, down the hall, and in the morning, you'll be taken to court to be arraigned." Swell. The holding tank was a small cell with gray walls and a couple of metal benches, which smelled like urine. Besides us there were already two other guys in there.

We kept saying that we couldn't believe that we had been arrested and were going to court in the morning. I don't think we slept a wink.

January 6, 1971, at seven a.m., the cop on duty told us that our bus was there and ready to take us to the Municipal Court of Orange County Harbor Judicial District. He cuffed us and brought us to the bus. About thirty minutes later we arrived at the courthouse.

When we got there, another police officer met us, took off our cuffs, and walked us into the courthouse. Even though it was early, the courtroom was already crowded.

Once we walked into the courtroom, he told us, "Sit down, don't talk, and wait until your names are called."

I had never been arrested before, so I was anxious, nervous, and scared. I looked at Larry and Tom, who also looked the same way. About an hour or two later, our names were called. We walked up to the judge's bench, and the bailiff read the complaint. It said that we took the personal property of El Rancho Market, consisting of meats and cheese. We tried to tell the judge that it was only one pack of cheese, a pack of chopped meat, and some hamburger rolls, but the bailiff told us to keep quiet. "Nobody asked you to talk."

The judge set our bail at a couple of hundred dollars for each of us.

Tom said, "Your honor, we don't have money for bail."

The judge said, "In that case, you'll stay in our custody at the Orange County jail. In a week or two you'll return to be sentenced." The officer then brought us back to the bus and put the cuffs back on us.

Once we arrived at Orange County Main jail, we were brought to a room where there were several cops. The guy at the desk was given our paperwork by the cop who brought us in. After they took off our cuffs, we were given orange jumpsuits, flip flops, and paper bags to put our street clothes in.

I couldn't help thinking what jerks we were. All this because we wanted cheeseburgers. Unbelievable.

After we changed into these orange jumpsuits, they handed us each a blanket, a towel, and a pillow, and told us to wait. About twenty minutes later, an officer walked us to the cells where people who were waiting to be sentenced stayed.

Larry and I were assigned to the same cell. It was a large cell with about seventy guys. Tom was in the cell below us. Before we walked in, the guard told us which beds were ours.

The cell was about a hundred and fifty feet long and thirty feet wide. It had a bathroom and a TV room at one end, and the rest of the room was filled with beds. Along the side with the bars were single beds; opposite them were bunk beds. The cell was completely filled. As we walked in, everyone was staring at us and making snide comments.

I just looked down, walked to my bed, and sat down with the blanket covering me. I didn't sleep well that night. Was this just a bad dream?

I had a single bed. There was a guy in the bed next to mine who didn't look friendly. He looked like he was Mexican-American, about 5'5", with greasy black hair.

The next morning, I learned that getting out of my bed on the correct side was very important. When I woke up, I could have gotten out of my bed on the left or right. I didn't think it mattered, but it did. I got out on the right side, and this guy immediately jumped out of his bed, walked up to me, got in my face, and yelled at me, "Get the fuck out of my space and never, ever get out on my side." He repeated that several times and walked away.

I was a little shaken up by this encounter. I guessed that since his bed was the first bed and since it was against the wall, the only way he could get out of his bed was to get out on the left side, which was my right side. I was thinking that I just woke up literally on the wrong side of the bed. That was the last time I did that.

That day, when I walked around the cell, whenever I saw my neighbor, he always had several guys with him. Some guy came over to me and said, "Your neighbor is the head of the gang in this cell. Watch out." I was sure I was going to get jumped either later that day or that night. The whole day I kept looking over my shoulder. That night, again I couldn't sleep. Any sound made me jump.

The next morning, I made sure to get out of bed on the left side. At six-thirty a.m. a guard would start yelling at us to wake up. He also called out the names of the guys who were going to court that day. We'd line up, single file, and without talking, walk to the cafeteria. It was large, with several metal tables and metal benches. When we got there, we were told which table to sit at. Once everyone was there, they started calling each table to get their food. All the utensils were plastic, and the food was almost inedible. The coffee was the worst I ever had. After breakfast we'd get back in line and return to our cell. It was the same routine for lunch and dinner.

Since we weren't let outside, there wasn't much to do. We could watch TV or sit on our beds and read whatever magazines we could find. Larry and I spent a lot of time talking about what we thought would happen to us. Across from our cell were cells that were called the "knick-knack rack." It was where the child molesters, rapists, and perverts were held, with only one guy to each cell.

The second day, while I was reading a magazine on my bed, some guy, about 6'5" with long blond hair, came over to my bed, sat down, and asked me what I was in for. All I could think of were those grade B movies about jail where some guy is befriended by another inmate and then gets jumped and raped, so I tried to act tough so he wouldn't mess with me.

I told him, "I'm in for robbery. Me and a couple of my buddies got caught stealing meats and cheese and stuff from supermarkets in Newport Beach."

He said, "I never met anyone who did that."

I responded by saying, "Well, now you have." I asked him why he was in.

"I was busted for dealing several pounds of heroin again, and since it's my second time being busted, I'll probably get several years if convicted."

When he found out I was from New York, he said, "I always wanted to go to New York City. What's it like?"

We talked for hours. He grew up in Southern California, played football in high school, and was an interesting guy. So instead of being abused by him, we became friends and talked every day. One good thing about having him as a friend was that my neighbor and his gang stopped giving me evil looks and didn't bother me the whole time I was there.

At the end of the week our names were finally called to appear in court. I was excited and relieved to leave but worried about what would happen next.

Before I left, my new friend came over to me and asked me for my address. He said, "When I get out, I'd like to visit you."

I told him, "That would be great," but he never did.

We were told to take our stuff and were brought to a room where we were given our street clothes and our release forms. Once we were dressed, they cuffed us and led us to a small bus that already had a few guys in it.

When we got to the courthouse, our cuffs were removed, and we were again led into court.

What would happen next? I was beginning to sweat.

Finally, we were called. We stood in front of the judge as the bailiff read the complaint to him. This time the judge asked us what the complaint meant, "Taking the personal property of El Rancho Market consisting of meats and cheese."

When he heard what we stole and why, he laughed. He looked at the bailiff and shook his head. He said, "I can't believe you were in jail for a week for something like this." He said he'd let us go with time served but suggested that we get out of Newport. He said, "Once you've been arrested, especially in Newport Beach, there is a good chance that you'll be arrested again." He also said, "You guys stand out with your curly hair and your New York accents." He might have just been saying that to scare us, and to his credit, he succeeded.

We left the court, hitched a ride back to our hotel room, and decided to take his advice and get out of town.

We decided that we'd continue our trip and go to Florida, maybe find a place in Miami Beach and live there for a couple of months. Since we had a friend who lived in North Miami, we figured we'd visit him and see if he knew any place we could rent. Along the way we could stop in New Orleans and party a little since it would be Mardi Gras when we arrived.

We called the car service that Larry and Tom used to get the car they drove to California. We got lucky. They said that in a few weeks they'd have a car that needed to be driven to North Miami. After hearing that we notified our landlord, our friends, and our next-door neighbor Bones that we were leaving in a few weeks.

When the car was available, we left Newport Beach and arrived in New Orleans two days later. We only stopped for gas, food, and the bathroom. Once we got there, we decided to sleep in our car and use our money, which wasn't much, to party. It was a lot of fun. Every morning we'd wash up at a gas station around the corner from where we had parked. After a couple of days, we headed to Florida.

Fifteen
Miami Beach

Since it took close to twelve hours to drive to North Miami, we left early. When we arrived, Tony was happy to see us and had a refrigerator full of cold beer waiting for us. We sat around drinking, telling him about our adventures in Newport Beach. When it started getting late, we decided to drop the car off. Since it wasn't necessary for all of us to go, Larry and I decided we'd drop it off and take a bus back.

The owner was excited about finally getting his car. Larry told him, "We plan on taking a bus back to our friend's apartment. Is there a bus stop around here?" We told him where Tony lived, and he said, "There's a bus stop just a couple of blocks away that'll take you a few blocks from there."

Maybe because we were tired from driving, or maybe because we had had a few beers, Larry and I got on the wrong bus, but we didn't know it until it was too late. What a couple of schmucks.

We knew we had taken the wrong bus when the bus driver said, "Last stop, Collins Avenue, Miami Beach." Collins Avenue was the main strip in Miami Beach. It may be hard to believe, but we didn't have enough money to take a bus to get out of there. Collins Avenue ran parallel to the ocean, with a beautiful white beach in between them.

When we called Tony didn't answer. He was probably out picking up some food for dinner. So, after a little while we called again but again, he didn't answer. We continued to walk along Collins Avenue enjoying the warm air and the sound of the ocean wondering what we should do. We called one more time with the same results. We were stranded. It was getting late. So we decided to sleep on the beach and try to reach him in the morning. We actually thought that sleeping on the beach, under the stars with the sound of the waves, didn't seem like such a bad idea and was allowed.

Eventually we found an area on the beach by a wall that would serve as a good cover, and no one could see us or bother us. Luckily, we were wearing jackets that we could use as pillows.

The next morning, at the crack of dawn, the sun woke us up. We put on our jackets, hopped over the wall, and started looking for a pay phone.

Suddenly, a cop pulls up to the curb, rolls down his window, and asks us what we're doing. Before we could answer, he got out of his car and walked over to us. He asked us, "Do you guys know sleeping on the beach is prohibited?"

I said, "We weren't."

With a knowing look, he asked us how we managed to get sand on our jackets. Without waiting for an answer, he asked for our IDs. After looking at them, he again told us that it's against the law to sleep on the beach and threatened to arrest us if we didn't get off Miami Beach immediately. After being in jail in California, being arrested again was the last thing we wanted.

There are several bridges that attach Miami Beach to the mainland, Miami proper, so Larry and I immediately found one and crossed it. As soon as we got to the other side, another cop car pulled up. I was getting nervous and didn't like what was happening. He also asked us for our IDs and said that he had heard on his radio that one of his buddies already stopped us. He wanted to know where we were going. I got the feeling we weren't welcome. We told him we were trying to get in touch with our friend who lived in North Miami and whom we'd be staying with. He asked us if we had jobs. Larry told him, "No, we just arrived from California where we were collecting unemployment." I'm not sure why he told him that, but the cop got annoyed and said, "You better call your friend right away and get the hell out of here. If I see you again, I'll arrest you."

Luckily for us there was an International House of Pancakes restaurant right across the street that had a pay phone. As soon as we got there, we called Tony but again no one answered. We started to think that maybe his phone was broken.

We sat down at a table, ordered coffee, and tried to figure out what we were going to do. Even if we got directions to Tony's place, we couldn't leave the restaurant now. It always seemed to be something.

After having a couple of cups of coffee that we didn't have to pay for since refills were free, I went to the bathroom. As I was washing my hands, I looked out the window above the sink, which looked out onto a parking lot. In one of the cars was an old guy who was waving at me to come over. I thought he was a pervert. I went back to the table and told Larry about this guy. He suggested that, "Maybe you should find out what he wants. Since he has a car, maybe you could talk him into giving us a ride." What a great idea.

I left and walked over to his car and asked him what he wanted. To my surprise, he said, "I have a janitorial service that cleans the local Loews movie theater on Collins Avenue, and the guy who has been working for me just quit. I need help. Do you want a job?"

I couldn't believe he was offering me a job. I told him that I was with my friend and asked if he needed two helpers, but he said, "I only need one."

I asked him, "If I take the job, would you give my friend a ride to our friend's apartment?"

He said, "Yes."

I ran back into the restaurant and told Larry what this guy had said. In fifteen minutes Larry was at Tony's apartment, and I was heading to my new job. Before Larry got out of the car, I had this guy give him the address of the theater and what time I'd be done so that Tony could pick me up when I was done working.

On the way to the theater, my gut feeling was that this guy was on the up and up. He told me what my job was. I'd sweep the floors, vacuum the carpets, and clean the bathrooms. I only had to work four hours a day from eight a.m. to noon five days a week. I would get $1.60 an hour, paid every Friday. Also, if I liked buttered popcorn and soda, I could have as much as I wanted. Since I loved buttered popcorn, that sounded good to me.

When I was done working, Tony, Larry, and Tom picked me up. The first question I asked Tony was "Why didn't you answer your phone?"

He said, "It's broken."

Our plan was to find an inexpensive place to live on Miami Beach for a couple of months. So we drove down Collins Avenue looking for a place. It wasn't long before we saw a sign, "Room for rent," at the Claridge Hotel right on Collins Avenue, across from the beach, just down the road from the Fontainebleau Hotel.

In the other direction was South Beach. We didn't know this at the time, but Miami Beach was a retirement community, and the people that lived there didn't like our type. No wonder the cops were harassing us. The Claridge Hotel was nice. The place had a kitchen, a large bedroom with three beds and three dressers, and a bathroom with a shower. The price was right, so we took it. We couldn't believe how lucky we were to find a place right away that was right across the street from the ocean, just like in Newport Beach.

Every morning I'd get up at seven, put on shorts, a tee shirt, and flip flops, and walk or hitch to work. Every day was warm and sunny.

One morning I was walking by the Fontainebleau Hotel on my way to work, and in the parking lot I saw one of my idols, the heavyweight champion of the world, Mohammed Ali, stretching and shadow boxing. He was probably getting ready to do some road work for his fight with Joe Frazier that was in March at Madison Square Garden. It was billed as "The Fight of the Century." He worked out of a gym in Miami Beach.

I was so excited to see him that I yelled out, "Good luck, champ." Normally I wouldn't do that, but it was Mohammed Ali. He waved and said, "Thanks." I couldn't believe he responded. What a way to start my day. For the rest of the day I was on Cloud Nine.

Most days, when I arrived at work, I'd start by having some buttered popcorn and soda for breakfast.

One day when I was walking home from work, I saw a sign at the Montmartre Hotel, one of the many hotels on Collins Avenue.

They were looking for a lifeguard and a SCUBA instructor to work from one p.m. to four p.m. The time worked perfectly. Since I could swim, and since my father was in a SCUBA club, I figured I'd apply. After talking to the hotel manager, I got the feeling he wasn't looking for a certified lifeguard or a certified SCUBA instructor but someone to act as a "babysitter" for the guests' kids. He seemed satisfied that I had worked at Jones Beach and knew that SCUBA was an acronym for Self-Contained Underwater Breathing Apparatus.

He needed someone right away since the hotel was filled with families, and the guy who held the job was sick and didn't know when he'd return.

After asking me several questions, he said, "You got the job. Can you start tomorrow?" "You bet." Then he introduced me to the assistant manager and a woman at the front desk as their new lifeguard. The manager was friendly and very appreciative that I took the job. He told me that if I wanted lunch, I could just ask the assistant manager and he'd get it for me… for free.

The next day, as soon as I got there, I changed into my bathing suit in a cabana that was assigned to the lifeguards. Kids were running around, jumping in and out of the pool. As I circled the pool several of the parents came up to me and asked me to throw-an-eye and watch their children, and they tipped me to do this. It was an easy job, and I liked doing it. Luckily, no one was interested in SCUBA instruction.

A couple of weeks later, Tom got a job as a cabana boy at the Barcelona Hotel, but Larry never got one. Once a week he'd join me for lunch sitting by the pool. While we had lunch, I kept an eye on the kids. After lunch Larry left, and I resumed walking around the pool schmoozing with the parents.

Since Tom and I were working, we finally had some money to go out for dinner to some of the local coffee shops like Sambo's or Wolfie's, two popular coffee shops in the area. After dinner we'd walk along Collins Avenue and sometimes visit one of the nicer hotels like the Fontainebleau to have a drink and try to meet girls, which we weren't successful at, but we had fun trying.

Vacation in Freeport, the Bahamas

One Saturday afternoon, while sitting around our apartment, Larry got a letter from his parents with a check in it. It was a check for all the money he'd been sent from the unemployment office in Newport Beach. It seems that instead of sending his checks to our address in Newport Beach, the checks had been sent to his parents' house in Levittown.

The check was for several hundred dollars. That night, while eating dinner, we talked about what we'd do with our newfound wealth.

Instead of being responsible and maybe holding on to it, we decided to visit a travel agent the next day and book a long weekend vacation in Freeport in the Bahamas. Of course, going on a vacation was ridiculous, but the whole trip had been taking on a surreal feeling.

A week later we were in Freeport. Once we checked in, we changed into our bathing suits and went to the pool. While at the pool we met three Canadian nurses. They were very friendly and cute, and most importantly, they wanted to hang out with us. We told them that we were in a band and were on vacation since we just got through touring and needed some down time. We said that we didn't want to mention the name of the band because we didn't want people to bother us. Which they respected or they didn't care. They were smart and a lot of fun. At night we'd all go into town, have dinner and a few drinks, then return to the hotel and sit by the pool or take a walk on the beach. After a couple of days, we told them that we had to return to Miami Beach to work on a new album.

A Surprise Visitor

One sunny afternoon after work we went supermarket shopping. While we were returning to our apartment, one of our next-door neighbors from Newport Beach came running up to us out of the blue. We were very surprised to see him.

Larry asked him, "What are you doing here and how did you know where we were?"

He said, "You told me you were going to Miami Beach, and that was all I needed to know." He said, "I was getting tired of Newport Beach and decided to join you guys." He said that he'd been walking around for a few days looking for us and was glad he finally found us. We were dumbfounded and couldn't believe he had found us. He asked us, "Can I stay with you?" He was a nice guy, and since we had a couch that he could sleep on, we said, "Of course."

He was an interesting guy who had been a top gymnast in high school and was going to try out for the 1972 Olympics. He was given a full scholarship at some college, but unfortunately in his freshman year, while training, he hurt his shoulder. He said, "The doctor said that it was a severe tear to my rotator cuff and would take at least a year, maybe longer, to heal, and he didn't think it would be fully healed in time for me to train and try out for the Olympic trials." Since he was on a sports scholarship, the college told him that they would have to cancel his scholarship. His parents couldn't afford to pay for college and he didn't want to go back home, so he decided to go to Southern California, where we met him.

One day while I was working at the hotel, he joined me for lunch. While we were eating lunch, he asked me, "Would you like to see some of my moves off the diving board?" He added, "Besides being a gymnast, I was also on the diving team."

He climbed on the diving board and did some incredible dives. He'd do summersaults and twists just like they did on the Wide World of Sports on channel seven. Everyone around the pool stopped what they were doing and watched him. After a few dives everyone started clapping and hooting. It was very cool. After he left, several of the guests asked me if he was going to be the noontime entertainment.

A couple of weeks later he got a job doing that at another hotel.

Every day was warm and sunny. It was a nice life, but after several months I was thinking of returning home. Just around this time our friends from Long Island drove down to visit us. They were on their spring break. It was great to see them. After work they'd come over to our apartment, have a couple of beers, and then we'd go somewhere and have dinner. We got to know Miami Beach well and went to different bars every night. After a week they decided to return to Long Island, so Larry, who also planned on returning to Long Island, and I decided to leave with them. Tom stayed.

I said goodbye to the guy I worked with at the Loews Theater. I told him I'd never forgotten how he saved me and my friend, and how much I enjoyed working with him. He seemed surprised to hear that and touched. I also said goodbye to the manager at the Montmartre Hotel, who thanked me for stepping in and helping him when he needed someone desperately. He told me that he'd always have a job for me. Good to know.

Sixteen
Finding a Job in New York City

After returning from Miami Beach, I went back to work at Jones Beach. It was still a good job and seeing the guys was great, but I was getting tired of the work and decided it would be my last summer there. I wanted to move into the city and get a "real job."

Once or twice a week, after work I'd change my clothes and take the Long Island Railroad into the city and look for a job. I had a black folder in which I carried copies of my resume that I left at every agency I visited. With an optimism that I'd find a job sooner or later, I'd walk the streets.

I was looking for a job in advertising, but since I didn't know anyone who worked in advertising, I would randomly walk from office building to office building in midtown, usually on Madison Avenue, Park Avenue, or Third Avenue. I would look at their directory to see if there was an ad agency in the building. If there was, I'd go to the agency and ask the receptionist if they were looking to hire someone. I didn't care what the job was as long as it was in advertising. It was easy to get access to the agencies since security was much more relaxed back then and no one asked for my ID or where I was going. If security did ask me where I was going, it was only to help me take the right elevator. I'd spend all afternoon dropping off my resume and then return home. As the weeks dragged on, I became a little less optimistic and a little depressed thinking that I'd never get a job and never move into New York City.

Working in a Gas Station

That fall, with the end of the beach season looming, I still hadn't gotten a job in the city. My car, a green Triumph Herald with right-hand steering, always needed work and I got friendly with the owner of the gas station that I brought it to.

One day, while I was waiting for my car, Ozer, the owner of the gas station, asked me, "Would you like a job working here three days a week?" Since the beach season was almost over, I told him maybe. He told me he couldn't pay me much, but he would show me how to work on my car and wouldn't charge me for the repairs. He said, "You could help me by pumping gas and working on some of the cars doing simple things that I'll show you how to do." It sounded interesting and an opportunity to learn about cars, save some money on repairs, and make some money, so I accepted his offer.

I worked from eight to four and always had grease under my nails. Every day I learned something new: changing brake pads, replacing gaskets and hoses, how to take out a radiator that was leaking, and how to change and balance tires. I never thought that what I learned would come in handy, but it did on a future trip to Mexico.

On my days off I would go to the city and look for a job. Eventually, I got a job at E.T. Howard Advertising Company in their mailroom. I told Ozer I'd be leaving, thanking him for everything he taught me. Since I didn't want the responsibility of a car, I decided to give it to him.

The agency was small, about fifty people, with some good accounts: Penthouse magazine, J&B Scotch, Bombay Gin, and Minolta cameras. I'd take the train into Penn Station and walk to my job on Third Avenue at Fifty-First Street. I loved my job and working in the city. Within a few months I got a promotion. They made me a junior account executive, working on some of their smaller liquor accounts.

One morning when I was delivering the mail, one of the secretaries, who knew I was looking for an apartment, told me that her sister was moving out of her studio apartment on the Upper East Side and asked me if I was interested in it. The next day after work I met her sister to check it out. It was a fifth-floor walk-up on Eighty-Second Street between First Avenue and York Avenue. The rent was $170 a month, and I could walk to work since the agency was only thirty blocks away. The studio was small, about 300 square feet, with a kitchen that was barely big enough for one person, a small bathroom, and a room ten by thirty feet. It was recently painted. The view from the two windows in the back of the apartment was of other apartment buildings. All I cared about was getting an apartment, so I decided to rent it. I called the landlord the next day and signed the lease.

Once I moved in, I asked my girlfriend Barbara Reilly, whom I had been going out with, if she wanted to move in with me. She did.

One of the first things I did was to build a loft bed to give us more space. Using two-by-fours for the frame, a piece of three-quarter-inch plywood on top of that to support our mattress, which was dense foam rubber, and five-foot-long two-by-fours as legs. I anchored it to the wall and built a ladder and we were set.

Having a subway stop close to where you live is important if you live in New York City. Depending on the weather, sometimes I didn't want to walk to work, and since the art school Barbara went to was on East Twenty-Third Street, she had to take the subway, so having it close made life easier.

Working at City University of New York

One of the most memorable nights was when Barbara and I were sitting around our apartment with some friends, Willie, Geoff, and Tim, who worked at City University of New York at their central office, which was a couple of blocks from where we lived.

They said, "One of our friends is a manager at CUNY and is looking to hire someone. Would you be interested in the job?" I didn't know at the time that this job would change my life. I told them that I liked my job in advertising, but before I could tell them why, they asked me how much I was making. I was making sixty-two hundred dollars a year. They said, "If you worked at CUNY, you could make almost twice that, and the perks are amazing: twenty-five vacation days, twenty sick days, and sixteen legal holidays, and all this time is vested the day you start." Willie continued, "If you don't use this time, you can save it year after year with no limit."

I wasn't looking to make a career in advertising, so I told them I definitely would like to speak to their friend. They gave me his phone number, and I called him the next morning. After I introduced myself he said, "I already spoke to Willie. I'll meet you at a bar on York Avenue and Eighty-Fourth Street at five-thirty p.m. this afternoon."

Being interviewed in a bar seemed a little unusual, but wherever he wanted to meet was fine with me. When I met him, the first thing he said was "Ditch the tie." Then I gave him my resume, but he said, "I don't need to see your resume. If you're a friend of Willie, Tim, and Geoff, then you must be alright. You got the job." Wow.

That night Barbara and I took a couple of pizzas and two six-packs to their apartment to celebrate. Thanks, guys. The next day I gave my two weeks' notice to the advertising agency.

The new job title was Research Assistant. I had to collect data on the instructional staff at the eighteen colleges that made up CUNY. It was needed for reports that were submitted to the state and federal governments. I used a modem to dial into an IBM mainframe computer downtown, where I could access a statistical software package called SPSS that was used for both interactive and batched statistical analysis.

While working there I also learned about computers, programming, PL/1, Fortran, Cobol, what relational and hierarchical databases were, hardware, and networks. This knowledge led to an interesting and rewarding career in technology as a Project Manager at CUNY and beyond.

I worked at CUNY for eighteen years and accumulated so much time off that I was able to travel. I visited Egypt, Haiti, Paris, London, and Curacao. I also had enough time off to work at the 1980 Olympics. But most importantly, I worked with a woman, Iris, who introduced me to one of her friends who became my wife.

Seventeen
Trip to Mazatlán, Mexico

Prior to working at CUNY, I was still working at E. T. Howard Advertising agency. It was Christmas and a wonderful time to be in New York City. The city looked like a movie set. The streets were crowded with shoppers. Every store had Christmas displays and lights. Every other corner had Salvation Army volunteers with their red kettles collecting for the needy. Everyone seemed to be in good spirits. The first year we lived in the city we enjoyed celebrating Christmas in our new apartment. The second year we decided to go on a trip to Mexico.

A week before Christmas, the agency had a party. After the party Larry, my boss, and I went to his office to exchange Christmas gifts. He gave me three ties. I gave him a bottle of Royall Lyme cologne. He told me, "You can take the next two weeks off... paid, because it's usually a slow time." I was thrilled since Barbara was also on a Christmas break from school. We decided to take a vacation.

That night I told her about a town in Mexico called Mazatlán. It was on the west coast, and friends said it was like Miami Beach but a lot less expensive. Since Barbara also wanted to visit her parents, who lived in Houston, she was all for the trip. The border crossing that we were taking at Nuevo Laredo wasn't far from where they lived. We figured the trip would take about two weeks.

We decided to leave the day after Christmas. We packed my white BMW 700. I bought it from a guy I worked with to help him out. He needed money badly and quickly, and made me an offer I couldn't refuse. Even though I didn't think I needed a car when I first moved into the city, and I didn't, I really missed the ease of visiting my parents and friends and Barbara's sister and her husband who lived on Long Island. It was also a lot cheaper to go food shopping outside the city.

The day we were leaving finally came. We put our suitcases and a couple of duffle bags in the trunk, making sure not to forget the map we got from AAA (American Automobile Association) that mapped out the whole trip. We picked up some breakfast and hit the road. We couldn't believe we were really going to Mexico. We didn't make any arrangements about where to stay because we didn't have a schedule. We'd go with the flow.

We drove down the east coast, sharing turns driving, staying with friends along the way. We arrived in Houston several days later. We only stayed with her parents a couple of days.

Our plan was to cross the border at Nuevo Laredo and drive diagonally across Mexico from the northeast to the southwest to Mazatlán. We were looking forward to staying at some of the small, cute towns along the way and eating some "real" Mexican food.

As we crossed the border, we had the windows down, the glass sunroof open, and the radio playing. Barbara said, "It's the best trip I've ever taken." We couldn't stop talking about how much fun we were having…so far. With a dependable car and the map from AAA, the trip should be easy. Little did we know that we would experience some scary incidents.

As the sun started to set, we decided to stay in a town called Torreon. As we drove into town, we saw some restaurants, a small outdoor food market, some stores that looked like they were selling tourist stuff, a pharmacy, and a bodega. We pulled into the first motel we saw. The room was small and clean. After we washed up, we looked for a place to eat. A few blocks from the motel we found one. It had several tables, a radio playing mariachi music, and a few people at the bar. The restaurant turned out to be a good choice. The food was delicious, and the waitress, who spoke a little English, couldn't have been nicer. Saying that would become repetitious because every place we ate had delicious food, and the people were always friendly.

After dinner we walked around. The night air was intoxicating and smelled like flowers. For a small town it was busy with people selling stuff on little cardboard boxes on every corner. All the stores were open and were decorated with colorful lights outside.

Since the next town we were going to was Durango which was only a few hours away, we decided to stay in Torreon the next day and do a little shopping.

Before leaving New York, we had been given several warnings by the AAA. One was not to drink the water. They said, "If you drink the water, you'll probably get terrible diarrhea known as Montezuma's revenge."

As we were walking back to our room, we saw a street vendor who was selling tacos. Even though I had already eaten dinner, they smelled too good to pass up. I got two, and they were delicious. It was only later, while I was in the bathroom, that I remembered that they use water to clean the chopped lettuce for the tacos. Oops.

At three in the morning I woke up and realized I was a victim of Montezuma. I spent the next several hours running in and out of the bathroom. Barbara went to the front desk and asked the desk clerk if there was a pharmacy close. He said, "There's one around the corner that opens at seven a.m." At seven sharp she went to the drug store and returned with an over-the-counter anti-diarrhea medicine that they recommended. It did the trick, and later that day we strolled around town and bought some trinkets. I was feeling much better, and we were looking forward to leaving.

Early the next day we drove to Durango, which was known for being Pancho Villa's home state as well as for its scenic waterfalls and hot springs.

As we drove into town, we saw a hotel that looked like someone's hacienda and decided to stay there. It was only five dollars. The room was large, with cream-colored walls and a balcony with a small table and two chairs that overlooked a huge backyard with trees, goats, and sheep.

After getting settled we walked downstairs and asked the guy at the front desk if he would recommend a restaurant. He said, "There's one a couple of blocks from here that has a band and good food. You'll like it." He was right. The food was delicious. The band was so good that people were getting up from their tables and dancing.

After dinner we walked around town, but this time I wasn't tempted by the delicious-smelling tacos. On one of the dirt side streets we found someone selling leather stuff. Belts, pocketbooks, and cowboy boots. The boots were really nice; the leather work was beautiful. We both agreed that they were the nicest we had ever seen. Unfortunately, we didn't buy them, thinking that maybe we should wait and see if we would come across nicer ones that were less money in another town. It was one of our biggest regrets. We never saw nicer ones or cheaper ones the whole trip.

Unexpected Checkpoint

We got up early the next day ready for our next stop, Mazatlán. We were making good time; we rarely saw traffic. We couldn't believe that every day was as gorgeous as the last one. The sky was blue with no clouds, and the views were spectacular. Some areas were mountainous and other areas were flat. The ground was dry. It looked like it hadn't rained in a couple of weeks. We drove along talking about what we'd do first when we got to Mazatlán. We both were looking forward to checking in and then going to the beach.

Barbara said, "I can't wait to go for a swim and lay on the beach and relax."

Another warning by the AAA was to not bring any drugs into Mexico. Again, I didn't take this advice and had rolled several joints before leaving New York. I stored them in a plastic baggy that Barbara kept in her pocketbook, which she usually kept on the back seat.

While Barbara was driving, I took out one of the joints, lit it up, and took a few hits, getting high. I put the remainder of the joint in the ashtray which was in the middle of the dashboard.

I had just finished reading a book by Carlos Castaneda, *The Teachings of Don Juan*, that discussed shamanism and the teachings of the Yaqui Indians. As we drove through the desert, I thought that maybe being high in this environment might help me reach a higher mental level as was discussed in the book. What was I thinking?

We drove along, singing and enjoying the warmth of the sun with the sunroof open. We were trying to figure out which town we liked better, finally agreeing that Durango was nicer. All of a sudden, up ahead we saw a checkpoint, about hundred yards away. It had appeared out of nowhere.

We had been told that we might get stopped and that if they found any drugs, they could do whatever they wanted. Maybe put you in jail, or worse. They could walk you into the desert and shoot you, or they could rape your girlfriend. I was feeling anxious and scared. I leaned over and told Barbara everything would be alright, although I wasn't so sure of that. This wasn't good, especially with me being high and having half a joint in the ashtray and a bag with joints in Barbara's pocketbook on the back seat.

She slowed down and pulled off the road. The dust almost made the checkpoint disappear, but it didn't. When the dust settled, it was still there.

Once we stopped, there, standing in front of our car, was this guy about six-feet two, which was taller than most of the Mexicans we had seen, who looked like Clint Eastwood in the movie, *The Good, the Bad and the Ugly*, but wearing a police uniform. We figured that he was the officer in charge. He walked up to the car and told us to get out. Behind him, ten feet away, were about eight other guys with rifles. About twenty-five feet away was another policeman, a heavy-set man who was sitting on a chair in the shade. The uniforms of the guys with the rifles were light brown and wrinkled, but Clint's uniform was perfectly ironed. He wasn't smiling, and neither was anyone else.

As we got out of the car, he told me to take off my sunglasses and give him our IDs. He asked us, "What are you doing in Mexico?" He spoke English well enough for us to understand him.

“We’re on our vacation and we’re headed to Mazatlán.”

Then he asked Barbara to stand on the other side of the car. I figured he did this to see if our responses to his questions matched, but they didn’t.

Under the glaring sun he said, “Please open the trunk,” and told a few of the guys to check our luggage. They put down their rifles and started to open our suitcases and duffle bags. After shaking each item, they would drop it on the dusty ground.

After looking at our IDs he started calling me by my name. Instead of pronouncing it properly, he pronounced it as if it was three separate syllables: We-el-done. I didn’t correct him. He asked me if we had any “marywana,” which is how he pronounced marijuana. Of course I said no, even though my eyes were as red as a stop sign. I looked around, trying to act relaxed, as if nothing was wrong, which wasn’t the case. I was sure he knew I was high and was just playing a game with me, which he was winning.

After talking to me, he walked over to Barbara and asked her some questions. When he returned to me, he told me, “If I find any marywana, I’ll be very angry,” which I didn’t want. I didn’t say anything.

While this guy was scaring the crap out of me, one of his guys was bouncing the tennis balls we brought to play tennis when we got to Mazatlán. I guess he thought we might have hidden some drugs in them.

Once they finished going through our luggage, they moved to the front of the car. He asked me to open the hood. The first thing they did was unscrew the cover of the air filter. They took out the air filter and began shaking it and hitting it on the ground. The captain said, “It’s a common place for people to hide drugs.” Good to know.

They spent several minutes looking all over the engine, and then they looked under the car. After finding nothing in the engine, they opened the doors and started looking under the seats and taking out the carpets. While this was happening, again the captain asked me if we had any marywana, and he reiterated that if they found any, he'd be extremely mad, especially now that he and his men had spent all this time looking for it.

Several of the guys that were standing behind us with their rifles moved a little closer. I wasn't sure what to do.

As they looked under the seats, I was sure they were going to find the half-joint and the other joints. So I reached into the car and took the half-joint out and handed it to the captain.

He smiled. The guys stopped banging the carpets on the ground and watched him.

I told him, "I just remembered that I had it."

He asked me, "Do you have any more?"

I said, "No," although I wasn't sure if that was the right thing to say. My shirt was soaked with sweat and sticking to my chest. I'm sure the temperature was close to hundred degrees, but that's not why I was sweating.

He then asked, "Where did you get this, We-el-done?"

I told him, "I bought it in Durango, where we stayed the night before."

"How much did you pay for it?"

"A dollar." His smile had turned into something that looked suspiciously like a sly grin. Then he asked me, "Did they roll it for you?"

I said, "Yes," although I'm sure he knew the answer was no.

Without walking over to Barbara, he lifted the half-joint and asked her, "Where did We-el-done get this?"

She said, "He brought it from New York City."

I almost had a heart attack. He looked at me and then told the guys to stop searching. Luckily they stopped because the next area they were going to search was the back seat where the other joints were.

He told me, "Don't move."

Where was I going to go? I couldn't move if I wanted to; I was paralyzed with fear. He walked over to the guy who was sitting in the shade watching this whole scene. After a few minutes, although it seemed a lot longer, the captain came back and told his men to put everything back into our car. I had no idea what was going to happen next, but I didn't think it was good.

After they put all our luggage into the trunk without dusting off our clothes, they put the air filter back on and closed the hood.

He walked back over to me. I was shaking. He looked straight into my eyes, smiled, and said, "I believe you." I was shocked and couldn't believe what I was hearing. In a perverse way I wanted to hug him. Then he said, "Get back into your car and get out of here."

We got into the car. Barbara got into the driver's seat and asked, "What happened? What did he say?"

I told her, "I'll tell you later."

Before we pulled out, he walked over to Barbara, threw the half-joint on her lap, and said, "Have a good vacation."

We nervously said, "Thanks" and drove away.

Around two hundred yards down the road, when they were out of sight, I reached into Barbara's pocketbook, took out the baggy with the joints, and threw them and the half of joint out the window. That was more than enough excitement for us… At least, that's what we thought.

We couldn't believe how lucky we were and what a scary situation that was. We both agreed that now, even more than ever, we couldn't wait to get to Mazatlán and just lie on the beach.

But first we had to cross the Sierra Madre Mountains on a highway that I later found out was one of the most dangerous highways in the world.

The Devil's Backbone

I looked at the map and Mazatlán was about 140 miles away, which normally should take a few hours. But the AAA map said that it could take from five to seven hours, depending on traffic. That didn't make any sense. How could traveling 140 miles take that long, especially since the roads never had traffic? We soon found out. Not knowing what to expect, I decided to drive.

Unknown to us, this mostly-dirt road was considered one of the most treacherous roads in the world. It went over the western Sierra Madre mountains and was called the Devil's Backbone.

The road was the scariest road I had ever driven on. We were both very nervous from the last situation, and this one almost seemed worse. Again I tried to reassure Barbara that everything would be alright. She reminded me that my credibility was weak.

The road ascended and descended, with sharp hairpins and zigzag turns. In some areas there were cliffs and deep ravines that didn't have guardrails.

When I had enough nerve to look around, the views were breathtaking. The road was barely wide enough for two cars, let alone a bus or a truck. Sometimes, to get out of their way, I had to drive off the road and partially up the side of the mountain, then stop until they passed. The longer I drove the more terrified we got.

To add to our worries the transmission started to make noise. We tried to listen to music, but we couldn't. We were too scared. We couldn't even talk to each other.

I just concentrated on the road. Six and a half hours later, we arrived in Mazatlán. We were exhausted and drained by the day's events. Again we both agreed that we had had more than enough excitement to last the whole trip…again that's what we thought.

But as we'd find out, that wasn't the last unexpected adventure we would have.

We arrived in Mazatlán late in the afternoon and one of the first things we did was to drive to the beach. What a welcome sight. Before we even looked for a hotel, we parked on the Avenue del Mar that ran parallel to the beach and took a slow walk in the water. The water was warm and a beautiful blue-green color.

After about twenty minutes, we got back into the car to find a place to stay. There were several hotels across the street from the beach. We found one and told the desk clerk that we'd be staying about three days. The room was eight dollars a night.

Our room had a front window that overlooked the beach and the Pacific Ocean. The walls were a festive green, with several little Mexican drawings in frames all around the room. It was perfect.

As soon as we walked in, we dropped our bags and jumped on the bed and agreed how nice it was not to be in the car.

After a little while we decided to unpack our dusty clothes. We shook them out the window. It must have taken at least an hour to do this. Afterward we took a necessary shower. Then we got dressed and left in search of a bar to have a much-needed drink and dinner. We found a little restaurant where a guy was playing a guitar. My cold cerveza (beer) never tasted better.

Barbara had a gin and tonic. She took a sip and said, "I can't believe what we just went through." Amen to that. After toasting our survival, we took the advice of the waiter and ordered the local fish …the mahi mahi was delicious. We came to find out from him that just off the coast of Mazatlán, fisherman also caught swordfish, tuna and marlin daily. After dinner we were too tired to walk around town, so we went back to our hotel room. We'd check out the town the next day.

The next morning was beautiful. The bed was comfortable, and since we had left the window open, the fresh air was refreshing, we slept well. Knowing that we didn't have to drive anywhere was a relief. After getting dressed, we went downstairs and asked the desk manager to suggest a place for breakfast. The restaurant he suggested was only a few blocks away. We sat outside. I'll never forget what I ordered because to this day it was the best egg rancheros I ever had. Barbara said, "The omelet the waiter suggested was delicious, although I didn't know what was in it." After breakfast we walked down to the beach and relaxed on the sand.

The weather was sunny and warm, so after spending a little time sitting there, we decided to go back to our room, change into our bathing suits, and return with a blanket and towels. After going swimming, we couldn't stop talking about the day before. We wondered why the captain had said, "I believe you."

We were the only people on the beach, which looked like it went for miles along the coast. After a few hours we returned to our hotel, changed, and decided to do some exploring. Every night we tried a different restaurant and a different fish.

The next day after breakfast we walked to the town plaza to buy some fruit that we brought to the beach. We agreed that, in spite of our previous experiences, we were glad we took this trip.

After a few days we decided to leave and head up the coast, crossing the border in Nogales into Arizona, where we were going to continue our trip. Since it was going to take thirteen hours, we decided that we'd stop at a town along the way for the night and continue on our way the next day. Once we were in Arizona, we planned on visiting Frank Lloyd Wright's school, Taliesin West, first and then visit Paolo Soleri's home and school to see some of his urban-designed buildings and housing that he built underground. We also planned on buying some "Wind-bells" that Soleri made by digging holes in the ground that he used as molds for his bells.

After paying our hotel bill we packed the car, got gas, and left Mazatlán, driving north along the main highway, route 15 N. The Pacific Ocean was on our left, and on our right were farms and fields with cows or horses. As usual, there weren't too many cars on the road, so we were making good time. We talked about how excited we were about the next part of our trip. Little did we know what was next.

As I've mentioned before, we were warned by AAA about different things. Another warning was to be careful of cows or horses walking on the road since they weren't fenced in. When I heard this, I was sure that we'd see a cow or a horse walking down the highway and have plenty of time to stop or go around it. How wrong could I be.

We took turns driving. We listened to some Mexican music and stopped at a little stand on the beach for lunch. After lunch we continued on our way with Barbara driving. After a couple of hours we decided to stop at the next town for the night.

Soon I saw a sign for a town called Los Mochis that was about a quarter of a mile away. As I turned around to tell her that she should take the next jug handle into this town, I saw a large horse on the highway, about a hundred feet in front of us. Before I could warn her, as if she didn't see it, she hit it.

I was knocked out, but when I woke up, I assumed from the look of the car and the horse what had happened. We were probably going about sixty-five or seventy mph. Although Barbara swerved, she still hit it. After we hit it, it flipped up and landed on the top of the car, crushing part of the hood and the sunroof, shattering the windshield and all the other windows, and then rolled onto the trunk and off the back of our car, landing in the middle of the highway.

Barbara was screaming. She said, "Look at your face."

I looked into the cracked mirror, and my face was all bloody from the shards of glass from the smashed windshield. Luckily, before she hit the horse, Barbara was able to turn her head and didn't get hit by the glass so she didn't have any cuts.

The car was turned sideways in the middle of the road, with the engine still running. All I could think about was whether Barbara was ok. Once she said she was fine, I felt a little better although I wasn't sure if either one of us really knew how we were. As I looked around, everything was a little hazy. I wouldn't be surprised if we both had a slight concussion. Luckily, we were wearing seat belts, or it could have been much worse.

I got out of the car and saw the horse. It wasn't moving. It was dead. A couple of cars pulled over, and the drivers and the people in their cars got out and dragged the horse off the road.

I walked over to them and told one of the guys that we needed to see a doctor. He pointed to the town and said in very broken English, "I'll go with you to find a doctor." We all got into our car. This time I drove. With him standing on the back seat with his head and body sticking out the top of the car where the sunroof used to be, we headed for Los Mochis.

Now, this is where my experience working at the gas station paid off.

After going about a hundred yards down the road, the engine stopped. I couldn't stop thinking that this was all caused because we hit a horse. I rolled to a stop on the side of the road. I was thinking that it could be anything after an accident like that; in fact, I was surprised the car still ran. I was sure that even if I found what was wrong, I couldn't do much since I didn't have any tools. I undid the latch from inside the car, got out, and struggled to open the hood since it was smashed in.

When I finally opened the hood, I leaned over the engine. I was so nervous and sweating so much that my sweat was dripping on the engine. Besides having difficulty seeing, the sweat burned the little cuts on my face, but I figured that was the least of our problems.

I couldn't see anything wrong with the engine. The distributor cap was connected, the cables to the spark plugs were connected, and the cables to the battery were connected. I didn't see anything leaking, so I crawled under the car to see if I could see any problems there. Everything looked good. I continued to look at the engine feeling very anxious. About twenty minutes later, I thought I saw what the problem was. The fuel line that supplied gas to the engine was barely connected. I had my fingers crossed that this was the problem. I reconnected it, got back in the car, pumped the gas pedal a few times, turned the key, and it started. I felt a sense of relief…for the moment, not knowing what was next. I closed the hood, and we continued to Los Mochis.

We pulled into the parking lot of the first motel we saw. The guy who rode with us got out right away and told the manager at the desk that we needed a doctor and what had happened.

While I was signing in for a room, a police officer showed up. He wanted to speak to the driver. I'm not sure if it helped that the driver was a cute young woman, but he seemed extremely polite and courteous to Barbara.

While she was talking to him, a doctor arrived and checked me out. He used tweezers to remove the pieces of glass and then put salve on the cuts. As soon as Barbara was done talking to the police, the doctor checked her. He said, "I can't see anything wrong with you besides being a little shaken up. You're very lucky. I'll come by in the morning to see how you're doing."

I offered to pay him, but he refused. Before the guy who rode with us left, I thanked him and gave him some money that he gladly accepted. We couldn't believe how helpful, nice, and efficient everyone was. That night over dinner we couldn't stop talking about this trip and how it had turned into such an adventure.

The next morning, the front desk called and said the doctor was there. He came up to our room, and after checking us, he said we'd be ok and that I should keep applying the salve. After breakfast we walked over to the police station to see if we could leave since our car still ran.

The officer who spoke to us the night before greeted us and asked us, "How are you feeling? What can I do for you?"

I told him, "We'd like to leave," but he said, "You can't drive without a windshield."

I thought where am I going to find a windshield for a BMW? I was sure there wasn't a BMW dealer in Los Mochis. I wouldn't be surprised if they had never heard of a BMW, so that only added to my anxiety.

We left the station and walked around the town hoping to find any car dealer that could help us, which we didn't.

Barbara, trying to be optimistic, said, "We'll figure something out."

We both agreed that we wanted to get out of Mexico as soon as we could. Maybe there was a junkyard that had a piece of glass I could jury-rig as a windshield. We found a junkyard, but unfortunately they didn't have one. We finally found a small hardware store, and to our surprise they had a roll of heavy-duty plastic, the kind that my mom used to cover our living-room furniture to protect it. I figured I could probably use it as a windshield.

We bought three yards of it, a roll of duct tape, scissors, and two pairs of goggles. Within an hour we had a windshield and plastic windows, all taped in. It looked strange, but all we cared about was that it would pass their approval and they would let us leave.

We drove to the police station and asked him if this would do. He said, "It's not up to me to give you permission to drive like this. The only person who can do that is the local judge. He'd have to write a letter giving you permission to drive up the coast like that."

"Where can we find him?"

He said, "Normally he'd be in court, but since it's Sunday, he's either at church or home, and he doesn't like to be bothered on the weekend, especially Sunday."

But Barbara pleaded with him, and he agreed to drive us over to the judge's house. Luckily, he was home. When he opened the door, he looked annoyed. He was a small man who looked like he was in his seventies, and he was still wearing his pajamas and a robe.

The officer said, "I'm sorry to bother you, sir," and then explained to him why we were there.

The judge chuckled and told the officer that he'd write the letter. He closed the door and, ten minutes later, he came back with a letter that he gave us. Great.

The officer brought us back to our car and wished us luck. We checked out of the motel, packing up as quickly as we could, and left. The new windshield wasn't clear; it was a bit hazy, and wearing goggles didn't help our vision. I wanted us to wear them just in case the tape let go. Once I was happy that the tape was holding, we took them off, which made looking out the windshield a little better.

As I drove along, we both said how concerned we were about getting stopped at another checkpoint. Of course, as we said this, we saw a checkpoint. As I pulled over, the police captain walked over to us and told me to roll down my window and give him our IDs. I guess he didn't realize we didn't have real windows, so I got out and gave him our IDs and the letter. He read the letter and smiled. He yelled over to the other guys who had rifles, "They hit and killed a caballo." They all started laughing. He turned to me, handed me our IDs and the letter, said, "Vamos," and walked away.

Later that afternoon we crossed the border and were back in the good ole USA.

Most people, at this point, would say that they had had enough, especially with the condition our car was in, and go home, but not us. Since the car still ran and since our plastic windshield was still holding up, we decided to continue our trip.

While we were driving down the highway looking for a place to stay, we were pulled over by the highway patrol. The policeman walked over to our car shaking his head. He told me to get out and asked for my license and registration.

"What happened?" he asked.

I told him and he began to laugh, repeating, "You hit a horse!" After looking at my license and registration, he handed them back to me and said, "Be careful," then walked back to his car and drove away.

We continued on our way and stopped at a motel that was a few miles down the road. The next day after breakfast we visited Taliesin West. It was the winter home and school of architect Frank Lloyd Wright. It was in the desert, and with Wright's modern design, it made for an interesting contrast. After the tour, we drove to Paolo Soleri's school of architecture and ecology. After that tour, we bought one of his bells. Both places exceeded our expectations, and we were glad that we continued our vacation. Now we were ready to return home.

We decided to drive back to Barbara's parents' house since we didn't think the car would make it to New York. As it turned out, it lasted until we pulled into their driveway, where it finally died.

The next day we met with an insurance agent who said our car was totaled. No kidding.

We explained to him that we needed to get back to New York City for work and school, so instead of making us wait, he had his office cut us a check right away. As soon as we got it, we called the airlines and got the next flight to NYC.

Eighteen
Searching for an Apartment

A few months after we returned from Mexico, Barbara and I decided to split up. Neither of us wanted to stay in the apartment we had shared. She found another apartment quickly, but I didn't. Since I didn't have money to pay a broker, I had to find an apartment on my own. I had only two criteria: it had to be in Manhattan, and it had to be affordable.

At least three times a week, after work I'd go apartment-hunting. It was kind of exciting at first. I'd take a subway to different parts of Manhattan where I thought I might want to live. I went to the Lower East Side, Alphabet City, Chinatown, Little Italy, Tribeca, and the West Village.

I'd walk around until I saw an apartment building in an area that I liked. I'd walk into the lobby, buzz the super, and ask if them if they had an apartment for rent. This went on for months; it wasn't easy finding a place, especially since most of these places were out of my price range. I could probably afford them if I had a roommate, but I didn't and didn't want one.

After work, on a beautiful spring night, I decided to go to the West Village. I was feeling a little depressed about not finding an apartment, so this night I decided to visit a fortune teller.

As I turned the corner there was a sign: "Psychic, fortune teller." It was probably a waste of money, but I was getting desperate. I walked down a few steps and went into a small room that had colorful sheets hanging on the walls. It looked a bit like an Arabian tent. There were three chairs and a small table in the middle of the room.

The fortune teller walked into the room and said, "You look lost." We sat down and she asked me, "Where do you live and what do you do?" We talked for about fifteen minutes when she said, "Your time is up."

After I paid her, she said, "I have a feeling that your luck is going to change." As I walked to the subway, I was hoping that she was right.

The next night I went back to the same area. I started walking down Grove Street, a beautifully tree-lined street that doesn't look like the rest of New York City, and saw a sign in a window: "Apartment for Rent."

I rang the super's buzzer.

The super came to the door and asked, "What do you want?"

"I'm looking for an apartment and saw your sign."

She said, "Follow me. It's on the second floor, so we'll take the stairs."

The apartment had a long hallway that led into an area she called the kitchen-living room. It was a small one-bedroom apartment although the bedroom looked like a large walk-in closet. I loved it immediately, especially when she told me the rent…two hundred dollars. The windows in the kitchen and the bedroom faced Grove Street. I felt lucky to find an apartment in this area that I could afford and that was only two blocks from the subway.

After I moved in, my bedroom was so small that I could only fit in my bed and a small dresser where I put my 14" color television and a lamp. The bathroom was off the kitchen and was very small. One time when my father was visiting, he said, "It's the only apartment I was ever in where you could piss in the toilet and the kitchen sink without moving." It was that small. Only my dad would say that.

I had never lived alone, so it took some time to get used to it. I had a lot of free time and sometimes was a little lonely. I still had my friends from Hofstra who had also moved into the city and who I still hung out with, but something was missing.

Some days, to burn off some of my anxiety, I'd run along the existing elevated West Side Highway. I needed to be productive and find something else to take up my time, so I decided to paint. I had been an art major in college. To get back into the swing of drawing and painting I took some classes at the Art Students League.

Many nights, to pass the time, I'd sit looking out the window, watching the people walk by, wondering what everyone did.

I was trying to think of some way that I could replace this lonely, negative feeling with a positive feeling through my art. This went on for months.

One day, after going for a run, I came up with my vision. I thought since fire is one of the most negative things in our lives, I would use it to create something positive. I would make paintings by burning out an area of the canvas (negative) with an acetylene torch. The exposed wall behind the painting would become part of the painting (positive) with its textures and color.

I walked to Canal Street, about five blocks away, bought some supplies at Pearl Paint, and started stretching canvases. Every day when I got home, I couldn't wait to paint. I was feeling much better, and sometimes, when I was painting, I'd allow myself to fantasize about having an art show in Soho, which was only a few blocks away.

Several years later I heard about another artist, Lucio Fontana (1899 – 1968), who opened his canvas by cutting it or puncturing it, leaving distinctive gaping slash marks and holes. He started a movement called Spatialism.

After finishing several paintings, I decided to live my dream. I took pictures, which became slides, and put together a portfolio.

My process of trying to get a show was simple. If I was feeling confident, I would walk over to Soho and visit a few galleries. I'd ask them if they'd look at my slides, hoping that they liked them and would give me a show. There were galleries on every street, with West Broadway having some of the most influential galleries in the world. Some of the galleries liked my paintings but were concerned that opening the canvas with fire was compromising the canvas and it wouldn't last. Fifty years later they still look fine.

One evening my dream came through. The owner of Ward-Nasse Gallery on Prince Street called, saying, "I saw your slides and would like to include you in a group show I'm having."

It was a group show of ten artists. Each artist could only exhibit one painting. The opening day was a beautiful day, and the streets of Soho were packed as was the gallery. Several people told me they liked my painting and wanted to know when I was going to have another show. I wasn't thinking of another show; I was happy to be part of this one.

About a month later, the West Broadway Gallery called to say that they'd like to see my slides. The next day I dropped them off, and that night they offered me a one-man show. I couldn't believe it.

The time flew by and before I knew it, I was having another show. The gallery was packed. I exhibited six paintings. Everyone liked the uniqueness of the paintings. Several of my friends came in from Long Island, and when the gallery closed, we went to the Broome Street Bar to celebrate.

The next day, I went back to the gallery to hear what the response was to my show. They said, "We're happy to tell you that we had a couple of offers to buy a couple of your paintings."

After several months, the hallway in my apartment was so crowded with canvases that anyone who visited me had to walk sideways to get in.

I was pumped and wanted to start painting on larger canvases, but obviously my apartment was too small. I needed a larger apartment or maybe a loft.

Nineteen
The Loft on Crosby Street

One day, my friend Tim White, who was a writer for *Crawdaddy* magazine, told me that the magazine's softball team needed players and asked me if I was interested in playing with them. He knew that I played on the Jones Beach Employee League and would probably say yes, which I did. The next week he called me to say that the team was playing a game in Central Park.

The team was good. We won the game and afterwards, while we were celebrating with a few beers, I asked the guys if they knew anyone that was renting a loft. Peter Knobler, the captain of the team and the editor-in-chief of *Crawdaddy* magazine, lived in Soho on Greene Street. He said that his landlord, Sam, owned several buildings in Soho and might have one.

He gave me Sam's phone number, and I called him the next day. He said, "I have one on Crosby Street between Spring Street and Broome Street if you're interested. I can meet you tomorrow at five p.m.…ok?" The next day after work I took the Lexington Avenue local #6 to Spring Street.

I got there a little early so I could check out the area. Several of the streets including Crosby Street were paved with cobblestones that gave the area an old-time feeling that I liked. The neighborhood was deserted. The only people I saw were guys in trucks going in and out of these buildings with handcarts. It didn't seem like anyone lived around there. Several of the buildings had graffiti on them. Several years later, Basquiat also wrote his tag SAMO on several of the buildings.

After checking out the neighborhood, I met Sam. He was an older man and was wearing all black as he was Hasidic. Over the years he and I became friends. We'd talk about the changes I was making to my loft and how the neighborhood was changing. We even stayed friends after I moved out.

The loft was on the second floor of a five-floor building. The front door had graffiti all over it and didn't seem very secure. As we walked in, I wasn't sure what I was getting into. The entry hallway was dark, with a musky smell. The walls were gray or just a very dirty white, with one fluorescent light that was flickering. There was an elevator in the back of the hall that Sam said opened into each loft, but we took the stairs. As we walked in, Sam turned on the lights. There were only two fluorescent lights, one in the front and one in the back. The place was a hundred feet long by twenty-three feet wide, twenty-three hundred square feet, with a fourteen-foot ceiling.

I walked around, kind of surprised by its starkness as I had never been in an empty loft. The walls were brick. At one time they probably were white but now were dirty gray like the hall. There were windows in the back with a view of a building ten feet away. The front windows looked out onto Crosby Street and the fire escape. The bathroom only had a toilet, no sink, no bathtub, no shower. Outside the bathroom was a small sink. As I walked around, I heard rats running around in the pressed tin ceiling. The ceiling had several holes that the rats probably used to get out. The wood floors were beat-up and also had several holes. The loft had plenty of space but was far from what I thought was livable.

"It used to be rag factory," Sam said.

"What's a rag factory?"

"It's where the remnants of material from the fashion district, in midtown, get brought to, to be sorted, bundled and sold to other designers and gas stations." Sam said he had a rag factory on Greene Street a couple of blocks away.

There was stuff all over the floor. Several cardboard boxes, coffee cups, garbage bags, and a large metal tank lying on its side.

I asked him, "If I rent this place, will you clean this stuff up?"

"Don't you want hot water, Clears?" He never called me by my first name all the years I knew him.

"What does that have to do with you cleaning the place up?" I asked.

He told me that the tank was a water heater. I couldn't believe the loft didn't have hot water.

"It was a factory," Sam said again. "Any changes or repairs you want to make will have to be done by you, not me." Rent was two hundred and thirty dollars, plus two months' security deposit. "It's a good deal, Clears."

I thought that was a little high, especially considering all the work I'd have to do. I offered him less, but he said that he could probably get more and was giving me a break. He said, "I'll hold it for you until the end of the week." He asked me, "Do you have any friends that could help you fix it up?"

I did: my friend Charles "Wink" Winkler. I had met Wink at a party the year before, and we became good friends right away. He was a talented artist and one of the nicest, most interesting people I ever met. He had a ton of energy and a gravelly voice that I'll never forget. He was always up for a good time. We had several parties at his loft and apartment in Queens. Sometimes on the weekend we'd go to Englishtown with his sons Curt and David and his friend Ralph to see the Funny Cars race at Raceway Park, NJ. Of course, we always got tickets to go into the "pit area" behind the racetrack where they worked on the cars.

I was sure Wink would know how to do whatever I needed, like plumbing and hooking up the hot water heater or running wiring for electricity or connecting gas if I wanted to add another gas space heater.

Sam said, "Maybe you should have your friend come over and look at the space and then decide if it makes sense for you to rent it, considering all the work that you'll have to do."

He was right. Since I didn't have any money to hire someone, I'd have to do everything.

I called Wink and I told him that I needed him to check out this loft. He agreed to meet me the next night if I'd have a six-pack of beer and a joint.

He came over and wasn't thrown by the way it looked. He saw the loft's potential and thought that I should definitely rent it and said he'd be glad to help me.

The next day, I met Sam, dropped off the money, and signed the lease that he wrote on a napkin. No lawyers needed.

After I moved in, Wink came over and told me everything I needed to buy and how to hook up the water heater. I was thinking the sooner the better. After I moved in I took showers at an ex-girlfriend's apartment, but I didn't know how long that would last.

Moving in was easy since I didn't have much stuff. I took my paintings off their stretchers and rolled them up. My small dresser, television, the wood from my platform bed, and the foam mattress that traveled with me from my uptown apartment were all I had. A friend of mine lent me his truck, so I only had to make one trip.

Once I moved in, the nights were a little unsettling. Hearing the rats run around in the ceiling, thinking that they got out through the holes, was creepy and a little scary. Sometimes I wondered if this was the right move.

Living in the loft was a challenge and an unbelievable experience. But over the months and years, I had the opportunity, albeit necessity to learn how to do things to make this place a home.

Hot Water

Once I got all the tools and copper tubing I needed, I decided to connect the water heater. After several hours sweating copper tubing, I turned on the water heater and water began shooting out from every connection. What a mess. I called Wink who, after laughing, said that I used the wrong solder. The next week I used the right solder and finally had a shower.

Kitchen Cabinets

One summer I decided I wanted kitchen cabinets. I called several stores, but they all wanted too much money. I decided to call Wink and see if he knew anyone that sold inexpensive kitchen cabinets. He said, "No, but it'd be a lot cheaper just to make them... They're easy to make." He then asked me, "What are cabinets?" I had no idea why he was asking me this and how to answer him. After a few seconds, he said, "They're boxes with fuckin' covers on them!" He came over the next day, and we talked about what I needed to do to make them and hang them. I spent the whole summer "screwing and gluing," as he liked to say, making about ten boxes with fuckin' covers, attaching them with Swedish hinges. I also learned how to cover the doors with laminate. By the time I was done, they looked just like the ones I would have had to pay thousands of dollars for.

Finding Things in the Street

Since I didn't have much money, whenever I was walking or riding my bike around the city, I was always on the lookout for things I needed that were thrown out. If I found something too heavy to carry, I would get my dolly. One night I found a cast-iron ball-and-claw tub a few blocks from my loft. It must have weighed two to three hundred pounds. It was difficult rolling it over the cobblestone streets, but it was worth it. Finally I had a bathtub and a shower.

Refrigerator

One Saturday night as I was walking down Lafayette Street by the Public Theater, I saw a refrigerator lying next to the curb. I was only a few blocks from my loft. I was thinking that I wouldn't have to leave my milk, cheese, and orange juice outside on my window ledge anymore. I went home and got my dolly. All the way home I couldn't believe how lucky I was to find this. After I attached the door, cleaned it up, and put everything on my window ledge in it, I plugged it in. After an hour I checked to see if my milk was getting cold. It wasn't. It didn't work, but I really wasn't surprised. Who throws out a working refrigerator? Several months later, Gail's father gave me their old refrigerator when they got a new one.

Tin Ceiling

Having rats running around in my ceiling and getting out through the holes wasn't conducive to sleeping peacefully or having anyone over. But how do you fix holes in a tin ceiling? I found a store in Brooklyn that sold four-by-six-feet sheets of pressed tin ceiling with the same pattern I had. For several weeks, I'd take the subway there after work and buy one or two sheets. It was a hassle traveling with them on the subway, but I got used to it, and after a couple of months I was done. I still heard the rats, but I felt a little safer. After I got two cats, called Sushi and Sashimi, the sound went away.

Shoji Doors

One of the biggest challenges was trying to keep the loft's openness and let the light in from my front windows. My bedroom was in the front of the loft, and to give me privacy when friends stayed over, I built three Shoji screens eight feet high and two feet wide, connecting them with piano hinges. They were attached to a sliding track that I attached to the ceiling. I made them because they could be easily opened or closed, and because the white paper was translucent, so when they were closed, they still let light in.

Optical Illusion Kitchen Ceiling

I also wanted to define the ceiling in my kitchen. Of course, it was obvious it was the kitchen because that's where the sink, the stove that a friend gave me, and the refrigerator were, but I wanted to do something else to delineate it from the rest of the loft.

I had heard about a simple, inexpensive way to create a black tile optical-illusion ceiling. After attaching furring strips to the walls around the kitchen area, two feet below the ceiling, I hammered in small nails every eight inches that stuck out a little. I painted the strips and all the light fixtures in the ceiling above the strips flat black. I attached white strings to the nails, crisscrossing them, which created eight-by-eight-inch squares. When the lights were turned on, the string looked like white grout, and the empty squares looked like black tiles. It was a great optical illusion.

Space Heater

The loft was heated by a large, 50,000-BTU "Modine" gas space heater that hung from the ceiling in the middle of the loft. It faced the front of the loft and heated that area up first, but by the time it heated up the back of the loft, the front was cold again.

In the winter I wore a jacket to paint since my studio was in the back. I needed to get a second space heater, but I couldn't afford to buy one, of course.

One afternoon Wink called me from work. He was a fabricator and worked in the twenties on the West Side. He told me, "I was taking a cigarette break outside the shop when I saw some guy walking down the street dragging a large space heater. I asked him, 'What are you doing with that?' 'I'm trying to sell it.' 'How much do you want?' 'Fifty dollars and a pack of cigarettes.'" He saw that Wink had a pack in his top pocket. Normally these heaters went for hundreds of dollars. It was very unusual to see someone dragging a space heater around the city. Wink didn't ask him where he got it as he figured it was stolen from the subway. He knew I wanted another space heater, so he didn't hesitate and bought it while also giving this guy his pack of cigarettes. He called me and told me about this guy and that he had just bought me a space heater and to come and get it. After work I hailed a cab and picked it up. That night, Wink came over. I gave him the money and a carton of cigarettes, and over dinner of pasta and sausages, he told me what I needed to buy and what I needed to do.

The next day I bought "black pipe, connectors, elbows, a shut-off valve, hangers, black pipe tape, and a couple of monkey wrenches." I was planning on putting it up in the back of the loft, about fifty feet from the other one. He and I hooked it up that weekend. What a difference it made.

After a lot of hard work and time I had a nice loft with a beautiful tin ceiling, a very large kitchen with a cool ceiling, a large bedroom, a large studio, and some furniture. I painted the whole place white, and it looked great. Over the years it was a great place to have parties also.

Twenty
Lighting Design

In between sessions of work on the loft, I finally started painting larger canvases and also experimenting with adding lights to the backs of my paintings in the areas that I had opened up.

One day a friend came over to look at my new "light" paintings. She liked them and offered a suggestion. "If you want to learn more about lighting design, there's a school in the West Village, The New York Studio of Stage Design, that was started by Lester Polokov, which you might want to check out." So the next day I called to make an appointment to speak to someone. I was told, "You'll be meeting with Lester, and if you have a portfolio of your artwork, please bring it." Lester was a well-known set, costume, and lighting designer who worked on several Broadway shows.

The next afternoon I met with him. He showed me around. He looked at my portfolio and said, "I like what you're doing. It's interesting and different." He asked if I wanted to go there and why. I told him that I'd like to learn more about lighting. A week later he called. "I've accepted you into my school in the lighting design program." Great.

I later found out that most of his instructors were professionals and worked on Broadway. The goal for most of the students that went there was to also work on Broadway.

While attending classes I met a lighting designer, Craig, who was designing lights for several shows. Whenever he was there, he would assist the lighting instructors. One day he was telling me how busy he was. "I have a show I'm working on at the Equity Library Theater on the Upper West Side and a show at a dinner theater in Hazelton, Pennsylvania." He said, "I gotta get an assistant." He asked me if I was interested in helping him, and I said, "Yes." I thought that it would a great way to learn and be fun.

We worked together for a few years. It was a very tiring time and a very exciting time.

When we worked on a show, sometimes my schedule got crazy. I still had my full-time job at CUNY, and after work, I'd meet Craig at ELT and work until one or two in the morning. Then I'd take the subway home, go to bed, and then get up at seven for work.

It was worth it. I'll never forget the feeling on opening night. It was exciting and so rewarding. After a while I met several actors who were also dancers that needed a lighting designer for their dance recitals, so I got busy designing for them.

One of the most exciting lighting projects we worked on was the West Village Halloween parade. Everyone who worked on the parade met at Ralph Lee's place; he was the creator of the parade. His loft was in the Westbeth Artists Housing in the West Village. We'd meet about two months before Halloween and discuss how we could make the parade better. His loft was filled with large masks of dragons that he made which were an integral part of the parade. Craig and I were responsible for the interior and exterior lighting of the Jefferson Street Library. What a special night.

Lighting design was a great experience. The knowledge I gained not only introduced me to a part of the theater I knew nothing about, but it also helped me with my paintings.

In 1980 I worked at the Lake Placid Olympics assisting the lighting designer on the entertainment and shows for the athletes.

59 Crosby Street, loft is on the second floor

WELDON CLEARS

Invitation to Art Show

Painting of Delmonico's on Wall Street

Playing softball for *Crawdaddy* magazine in Central Park

Wink and me taking a break

Gramps' houseboat

Michele, Judith, who was visiting from Haiti, and me

Halloween: Gail and me as "Vampires"

Halloween: Wink and me as “the Blues Brothers”

Twenty-one
Trip to Egypt

The day started as it usually did. I got up at seven a.m. and got ready for work. It was the time when you had to wear a tie to the office. I had my usual breakfast, coffee and two plain donuts, walked to the subway two blocks away, and took the #6 subway uptown. The trip usually took twenty minutes. I got off at the 77th Street subway stop and walked to my office on 80th and East End Avenue.

I was a research assistant at CUNY's central office. I liked the job. The only problem was that because I was paid once a month, budgeting was tricky. It seemed that after I paid all my bills I was always strapped for cash by the second week. I didn't even think of saving.

While sitting at my desk, trying to figure out what I was going to work on, my ex-girlfriend Kathy Wilson called. She was pretty, smart, and always positive. The first thing I asked her was if she was ok since she never called me this early. She said everything was fine, but she wanted to know if I wanted to go to Egypt. She knew I didn't have money, especially since it was the third week in the month, so I wondered what the joke was.

It was no joke. Kathy worked for Arthur Frommer, known for his books on how to visit places in Europe on five dollars a day. He had branched out and was selling complete travel packages including airfare, hotel, and tours. She said, "The flight to Egypt isn't filled, so Mr. Frommer asked us if we wanted to go." He also said, "If you don't want to go, maybe one of your friends does." She didn't want to go, so she decided to ask me. The cost was only $250. It covered the round-trip flight and the hotel for a week.

What a great opportunity. A trip of a lifetime, I thought.

She said, "The hotel you'll be staying at is right across from the Pyramids."

How could I say no? Unfortunately, I didn't have two hundred and fifty dollars. I would need to borrow the money, and the only person I knew that might be able to lend me money was my other ex-girlfriend, Barbara. She had just graduated from the School of Visual Arts, had gotten a good job as a graphic designer, and was doing well. After I got off the phone with Kathy, I called her. She said she would be glad to lend me the money, and I could come by that afternoon and pick it up. "Can I go?" she asked. She said that she had just finished an assignment and had some free time. I told her that it would be ok with me, but she would have to call Kathy and ask her.

All day long I couldn't stop thinking about seeing the Pyramids. Before I left work, I called Barbara to make sure she'd be home so I could pick up the money. She told me that she had spoken to Kathy, who said she could go. Great.

"You can tell me about it when I come over," I said. But that all changed when she replied, "You know, though, that I can't lend you the money since I'll need it for the trip."

"What!" I couldn't believe she was serious, but she was. I decided not to make an issue of it and to try to get the money another way.

The next day, after telling several people my story, they decided to lend me the money I needed.

A week later we arrived in Cairo. Once we got off the plane, everything there was different. The air smelled different and had a sandy color, and there weren't any skyscrapers. I couldn't believe how excited I was. There was a bus waiting for us that took us to our hotel.

Kathy was right. Our hotel was right across the street from the Great Pyramid of Cheops. Wow. I knew this was going to be an unforgettable trip, and it was.

The first morning after breakfast we met the other people on the Frommer tour in the lobby and got our itinerary. Our first trip was to see the Pyramids and the Sphinx. The three pyramids (Khufu, also known as Cheops, Khafre, and Menkaure) were about two hundred yards from the hotel. All we had to do was walk up the road outside our hotel. It was awesome to see them in person; they were much larger than I thought they would be. Once we got there, Barbara, Tony, who worked for Frommer, and I broke off from the group and decided to walk around on our own.

While we were walking around, several guys asked if we wanted a guide. At first we said no, but we finally gave in. This guy who was dressed in a galabeya, which is like a tunic, approached us saying that he liked Americans and would like to be our friend and show us around. His name was Mohammed. Of course it was. He seemed a little different. He didn't ask for baksheesh…money.

He was a wealth of knowledge and had a sense of humor. As we walked around the Sphinx, Mohammed pointed to a village in front of the Sphinx where he said he lived. It was about a quarter of a mile away. He asked us, “Would you like to come to my home and meet my wife and son?”

Barbara and Tony said ok, but I whispered to them, “Maybe it’s a trick, and he and his buddies are going to jump us and steal our money.”

They said, “You’ve been living in New York City too long and are too paranoid. Relax.”

When we got to his house, he introduced us to his wife and his son, who was four years old. The floors in all the rooms were dirt except for the room he brought us to. It had a carpet and several large pillows and a coffee table. It didn’t have any chairs. There was a window that looked out on the road we took to get there. He was very personable and a good host. We talked about New York City and what it was like to live there. He said he always wanted to go there and maybe move there. While we were talking, Mohammed took out a hookah and asked if we wanted to get high. It had six removable bowls. He put a small piece of coal in each of them. On top of the coal he put a piece of hash, and on top of that he put a piece of scented tobacco. After one piece of hash was smoked, he’d replace the bowl with another bowl. He offered us Coca-Cola, which he seemed proud to have, and his wife served it to us. After a few hours we decided to leave.

Mohammed then suggested several things we could do while we were there and said he’d be glad to be our guide, all this time not mentioning money.

He suggested that the next day we should go to Saqqara. It was the site of the oldest known pyramid, the Step Pyramid of Djoser, and massive sarcophagi of the sacred Apis bulls. He said, “You could take a cab or a bus, but I could rent camels to get there.”

Traveling by camels sounded like a fun experience, so we told him traveling by camels would be great. He said, "I'll meet you in the morning at eight a.m. outside of your hotel's gates. It'll take about three hours to get there, depending on traffic." I told you he was funny. "Don't forget to bring water."

Walking back to the hotel, we agreed that a trip on camels sounded unbelievable.

Trip to Saqqara

The next morning the front desk called to say that Mohammed was waiting for us. On the way out we each picked up a couple of bottles of water. When we met him, he was on a camel and holding the reins of three more camels. He showed us how to get on and off them. We mounted them and slowly walked up the road, passing the Pyramids. Then we crossed the road to the Sahara Desert. I couldn't believe we were doing this.

We picked up the rocking motion of the camels quickly. Sometimes we'd take a break to stretch and relax on the warm sand. Riding through the Sahara was surreal. We didn't see anyone during our whole trip. The only sound besides our talking was the sand blowing on sand; it was like a loud hissing sound. After about three and half hours we arrived.

The first thing we saw was the Step Pyramid of Djoser, where we took a break. After walking around the Pyramid, we went over to the see the sites where Apis bulls, which were worshipped and considered the most important sacred animals to ancient Egyptians, were buried. They were buried in large granite coffins. Our guide told us, "The sarcophagi weighed 70-80 tons."

We walked underground through intersecting passageways that branched off at regular intervals. The air was cool and musty. The tunnels were barely lit.

After a couple of hours of being blown away by everything we saw, we got back on our camels and returned to the hotel. What an amazing day.

Every day was warm and sunny. We visited the Cairo Museum that was having a Tutankhamen show that took up several floors. Another day we went to Khan el-Khalili, a famous bazaar, and bought some gifts, then had lunch at a restaurant that Mohammed chose. The food was delicious.

Some days, since the Pyramids were just up the road, Barbara and I would hang out by them. I did some drawings and watercolor paintings, while she walked around. I was thinking how cool it was to be there. "Who hangs out by the pyramids of Giza?" After a while we'd return to our hotel and sit by the pool. While floating in the pool Barbara pointed out that she could see the Pyramids of Giza… Amazing.

After a couple of days there, my wallet started to smell like camel dung. It was the money. I was told that the money smelled that way because they didn't recirculate it very often.

One night Mohammed took us to a very cool place for dinner called the Turigagogo Restaurant Night Club on Rue – Pyramides. The food was great, and the belly dances were the prettiest I ever saw, with beautiful eyes.

During the whole time Mohammed only asked for money when we did something that cost money, like renting the camels, which was three dollars a camel, or having dinner. Most dinners weren't more than four dollars a person, including drinks. We never questioned how much he asked for. If he was padding the cost of things for himself, we didn't mind. We felt it was money well spent to have our own private guide. But I kept wondering what he "really" wanted.

Sunday morning arrived, and it was time to leave. The front desk called to tell us the bus was there to take us to the airport.

I started packing, but Barbara wasn't. She was sitting in bed watching me.

"Why aren't you packing?"

"I'm not going."

I thought she was kidding, but after a few minutes she still wasn't packing, so I asked her, "What's going on?"

"I'm going to stay with Mohammed. He said he likes me."

I couldn't believe what she was doing, saying. I explained the obvious re: wife and kid, but she said she didn't care. I thought of a lot of things I could say, but I knew nothing I said would change her mind. I finished packing without saying anything more and left. I went downstairs and got on the bus feeling confused and a little bit numb.

The whole trip home I couldn't stop thinking about what had happened.

A few weeks later Barbara showed up at my office to say she needed to talk to me. We walked over to Central Park and sat on a bench. She said, "Mohammed wants to move to New York City, stay with me, and become a US citizen."

So that's what he wanted. She then asked, "Can you lend me some money for his flight?" I looked at her in disbelief, shook my head, and said, "No." I sadly walked back to work. It was years before I saw her again.

The first thing I did when I got paid was to give everyone the money they lent me and a little gift.

Barbara, Mohammed, and me at Mohammed's home down the road from the Sphinx and the Pyramids.

Resting in the Sahara Desert near the Step Pyramid of Djoser

Twenty-two
Trip to Paris

One hot August day, while I was wishing that I had an air conditioner, my friend Kathy called. She asked me, "Do you want to go to Paris?" I had just finishing reading a book about Mondrian and his life in Paris and was fantasizing about what it would be like to go there and have an art show, so it was perfect timing.

She told me how much it would cost, which included the flight and the hotel. This time I had the money.

As soon as I got to work, I asked my manager if I could take my vacation in a couple of weeks. "Sure, where are you going?"

"Paris."

"Cool."

I decided to try to get an art show there and started putting together everything I needed: slides of my paintings and drawings and an updated resume with my most recent art shows. I also made a list of small galleries I thought might give me a show.

The day finally came. I was leaving at ten a.m. from Kennedy Airport. Kathy had a car, so she drove me there. I was excited for two reasons: one, I had never travelled alone, and two, going to

Paris to try and get an art show was something I had never even imagined I'd ever do.

Eight hours later I was there. The hotel was in the Saint-Germain-de-Pres quarter. My room was on the third floor, small, and didn't have a view, but that didn't matter. I only planned on sleeping there. I planned on trying to get an art show and then seeing Paris during the day.

I woke up early the next day, full of anticipation and hope. I went downstairs, had breakfast, and started my journey. I took out my map and headed to my first gallery. When I got there, it was closed. No problem, I'd go to another one. But the next one was also closed. I went to one more, but it was also closed. Maybe they opened in the afternoon?

I stopped a woman on the street and asked her, "When do these galleries open?"

She said, "September."

September!

She said, "In August all the small galleries close, and the owners go on vacation to the south of France for the whole month."

I sat down on a bench feeling disheartened and foolish. I couldn't believe what a jerk I was not to know this. After beating myself up for a couple hours, I decided to make the most of my trip in spite of that.

Each day while having breakfast I'd plan where and what I wanted to visit. Paris was a great city to walk around. I visited every tourist attraction that I could. I went to the Eiffel Tower, the Orangerie, the Tuileries, the Centre Pompidou, the Louvre, and Rodin's Museum.

I had heard about a flea market in Clignancourt that had 2,500 vendors. I found out what Metro line went there, and in thirty minutes I was there. The place was huge. After going from stall to stall, I found one that was selling Beatle boots. They cost more than I wanted to spend, so I did the best I could to negotiate a lower price, which was hard since I didn't speak French very well. But to my surprise, they lowered the price.

After staying a little while longer, I returned to Paris and just wandered around. It was almost as exhilarating as New York City. The architecture, the landmarks, the galleries, the women – it was just like I pictured it. The weather was beautiful. The air didn't smell like New York City air, it smelled like it was scented. Since it was summer it stayed light till ten p.m. The nights had a romantic feeling. What a beautiful city.

Contrary to what some people told me about the French not being friendly, I didn't find that to be true. Whether I was lost aboveground or underground, people were always friendly and helpful.

A Night on the Seine

One night I went to a restaurant where you sit at whatever table has a seat available even if you don't know the other people already sitting there. While I was having dinner, a young Parisian who was sitting at another table with his friends leaned over and asked me if I'd like to join them. Of course, I said, "Yes."

They could speak English fairly well, which was great. It was tiring trying to explain myself in French. After dinner they said, "We're going to hang out by the Seine. Do you want to join us?"

As we walked along the Seine, I explained who I was and why I came to Paris. One of the girls, who I was checking out and who had beautiful brown eyes and beautiful dark brown hair, came over to me and asked, "Tu fais quoi demain?"

For some reason, I remembered that phrase from French class. She was asking me, "What are you doing tomorrow?"

I told her, "Je ne sais pas." I don't know. I didn't have any plans.

She asked me, "Would you like to go to the Palace of Versailles with me?"

I told her, "Oui, that sounds great!" and before I left them, I gave her the address of my hotel.

The next morning, the front desk called me. "There's a very cute young lady here for you."

Before we started our trip, we had breakfast. She suggested, "We should take a bus so that you could see the sights. It's much more interesting than taking the Metro."

Versailles was unbelievable, and to think someone lived there. It was more ornate than I had imagined. The tour took about two hours. It was incredibly informative. As we wandered around she held my hand.

The whole place was out of a storybook. After the tour we walked around the gardens, taking breaks to sit on the benches and talk. Sitting in these gardens, especially with her, made it very special. She was sweet, with a beautiful smile that made me smile, and she spoke English a little better than the night before. It was getting close to lunch, so we decided to leave and eat at one of the cafés by the Eiffel Tower. After lunch we went to the top of the Eiffel Tower. Then we walked over to the Tuileries Garden and the Musée de l'Orangerie, where they have paintings of water lilies by Monet that covered the walls.

After a full day of touring we were a little tired, so we went back to my hotel to clean up and relax and have a drink before going out to dinner. After dinner we strolled along the Seine. The next morning after breakfast, we started our day by going to the Georges Pompidou Center. Since the Louvre is close to it, we also went there. We walked all over that day, having lunch and dinner. After dinner, as we were strolling down the Champs-Élysées, she said, "I've had a wonderful time with you and will never forget it."

She gave me a romantic kiss and then said, "I have to go now."

I was a little surprised, but if she had to go, she had to go. I told her, "I'll never forget our time together and how much fun it was." I gave her my address and then I helped her hail a taxi, giving her some money for the taxi, and kissed her good night.

Ivan

After she left, I walk around the Left Bank looking for a place to have a drink. I picked the first bar I saw. A few minutes after I walked in I heard someone call my name. Or was it coming from the kitchen? If not, could another person have the same name as me? I was taken aback when suddenly Ivan, a friend of mine from Hofstra, came up to me and gave me a big bear hug. He was African American, about six-foot four and two hundred and fifty pounds, who had been on the football team. What a wonderful surprise to run into someone I knew.

He asked me, "What are you doing here?" but before I could answer him, he invited me to join him and his friends. As we were walking through the bar, he seemed to know everyone. He brought me over to a table with several girls and guys and introduced me to them.

"I went to college with this guy. This is Weldon." He told me that he had been working in Paris for a couple of years but didn't say what he did.

After a little while he said, "We're leaving. Do you want to hang out with us?" We went from bar to bar. Every place we went, people knew him.

At about two a.m. we went to a beautiful townhouse. As we walked in, the music was deafening. Everyone was dressed very stylishly. It was a very eclectic group. Again, Ivan seemed to know everyone. The women were beautiful and friendly. Ivan and I took the elevator up to the third floor where there were people playing roulette and baccarat.

After ordering a couple of drinks, we sat down on a couch where Ivan introduced me to another friend, "This is Jean, this is his place." Jean said, "Bonjour. If you're Ivan's friend, you're my friend." Then he pushed a bowl of coke over to me, gave me a rolled-up hundred-dollar bill, and said, "Enjoy."

Jean, Ivan and I talked about Hofstra and how some of the people we knew were doing and all the amazing things that happened our senior year. After a little while we went downstairs and joined his other friends who were dancing to some great music.

When we left, the sun was coming up. I think I was still a little drunk and high. I hailed a cab but not before thanking him for an unforgettable night. I told him, "If you ever visit New York City, give me a call." What a night.

I stayed in Paris for one more day.

Even though I didn't get an art show, I had a great time.

Twenty-three
Trip to Haiti

Michel, a friend who worked for the French Ministry of Education and was assigned to different countries around the world, was visiting me. At the time he was working in Haiti. Before moving there, he had lived in Lagos.

I decided to invite a couple of my girl friends to come over and do some things with us. I knew the girls would like him since he was French, interesting, good-looking, and smart, with a good sense of humor.

Michel told us about Haiti and the town where he was assigned, Jeremie. He said, "It's a small town at the tip of Haiti, relatively isolated from the rest of the island, 117 miles west of Port-au-Prince. It's called the city of the poets because of the numerous writers, poets, and historians born there.

"Would you like to visit me?" he asked. "In a couple of weeks it'll be Mardi Gras, and it would be a great time to visit."

That sounded like an invitation we couldn't pass up. We all agreed that we could take some time off from our jobs. Roseanne was a teacher and said, "I'll be on a break. I can go." Mary, who was a doctor, said, "I can take time off," so we decided to take him up on his offer.

Little did we know that it would turn out to be one of the most dangerous trips we'd ever take.

He said, "I have a house with four bedrooms and a staff of five, including a chef." We made our travel plans, and in a couple of weeks we arrived in Port-au-Prince.

When we arrived, Michel's friend Thierry, who was a doctor, picked us up at the airport and brought us to his house. He told us, "You can stay here until you go to Jeremie." His house was nice, with three bedrooms and a large living room. As soon as we got settled, he offered us drinks and hors d'oeuvres. He made a delicious dinner with blood sausages, not my favorite, and then he drove us around Port-au-Prince. He was a nice guy and a perfect host.

The next day he told us that there were three ways to get to Jeremie. "You can take a bus, but it's a rough ride since most roads aren't paved, or you can take a plane, or you can go by boat."

We all agreed that taking a boat sounded like a fun way to go. He said, "The trip only takes three to four hours going northwest in the Canal du Sud that leads into the Caribbean Sea."

The next day we decided to leave. Thierry drove us down to the dock and helped us to buy our tickets. The boat was named the *Arthemise* and made this trip twice a week. It was leaving that afternoon at five p.m.

Thierry told us, "Most of the passengers have families in Jeremie and take this trip to Port-au-Prince to do their supermarket shopping because Jeremie doesn't have a supermarket."

After we got our tickets we walked over to McDonalds and picked up some burgers and fries. We figured we'd have a little snack while we sat on the deck watching the sunset. At least, that's what we thought we'd do.

About fifteen minutes before the boat left, we said goodbye to Thierry and thanked him for his hospitality.

The boat was about 110 feet long, and the deck was jam-packed with passengers.

As we boarded the boat, the captain met us and told us that he preferred that the girls stay in his cabin during the trip. He said, "Most of the people on my boat probably never saw a white woman." Then he asked, "Did you ever hear of voodoo?"

We weren't sure why he was asking us this, but we nodded yes and asked him why.

He said, "These people believe in it, and they might look at them as a bad omen."

I guessed we weren't going to have our burgers and fries on the deck while watching the sunset.

He brought us to his cabin, which was right behind the wheel-house. It was very small with three portholes next to the bed, a dresser, and a bathroom. Before the boat departed, I left the cabin and stood on the deck, waving to the kids on the dock. The girls waved to the kids from the cabin. It felt like we were going on a mini cruise.

The sun was starting to set, and it was the start of a beautiful night. I went back to the cabin to join the girls.

About an hour and half later, the engine stopped. We knew that the trip took about three hours, so we knew we couldn't have arrived. I left the cabin and asked the captain what was going on.

He said, "It's just a little problem. We'll be on our way in few minutes." I went back and told the girls. Just as I was telling them this, the engine started up, and we were on our way again.

About fifteen minutes later, the motor stopped again, and again I went to see what was going on. But this time when I asked the captain what was happening, he told me, "The cable connecting the steering wheel to the rudder has broken."

"How long will it take to fix?"

He said, "I don't know."

"Did you radio it in?"

He smiled and said, "This is Haiti. I don't have a ship-to-shore radio. Most boats don't." He then said, "Once we don't arrive in five hours, they'll know something is wrong and they'll start looking for us."

I returned to the girls and told them what was going on.

The next morning, we were still floating around with no land in sight, and we were hungry. The girls couldn't stay in the cabin any longer, so the captain made an exception and let them go on deck. Some of the people were generous and shared their sugar cane and water with us. All day we just floated around without seeing land.

The next morning was one of the scariest times I've ever had.

While the girls were sleeping, I left the cabin. I was sitting on the bow, half-asleep, watching the sunrise and wondering when we would be found, when I heard a sound.

The captain was walking around the deck with everyone following him and chanting. I noticed he was shaking something above his head. As they got close to the bow, they stopped. Many of them were looking at me with an angry look. The captain started chanting something and then took what he was carrying and threw it into the water. Everyone dispersed.

I called, "Hey, Captain, what's going on?" but he ignored me and walked away. Normally he was a friendly guy.

I didn't have a good feeling about this and wondered what that was all about.

About an hour later I walked over to him and again asked him what was going on. This time he told me. "Last night everyone got together and met with me to discuss their situation and their need to return to their families." He said, "They feel that the white people caused the boat's mishap and that the only way to get rid of this 'curse' was to throw you overboard. Luckily for you, I was able to convince them that I could capture your souls in a bottle, and by throwing the bottle overboard, it would be the same as throwing you overboard."

Good thinking.

He then said, "I don't know how long that'll work."

As he walked away, I just stared at the Caribbean Sea feeling a little panicky and helpless.

The first thing I thought of was whether I should tell the girls. About a second later I decided not to tell them. What good would that do? I prayed that we would be found…soon.

Within a couple of hours my prayers were answered. Some guy in a hollowed-out tree-trunk canoe found us. After talking to the captain, he left. In a few hours, he was back with a bigger boat that towed us to the dock in Jeremie.

When we got to the dock, Michel was waiting for us with a big smile. It was great seeing him. He helped the girls with their luggage and said, "You were on the news. It said that three Americans were lost at sea on the *Arthemise*."

That night over dinner, I told Michel and the girls what went on that morning and what I thought might have happened if we weren't found, but thanks to the captain, it didn't.

Roseanne said, "Not telling us was the best thing you could have done. We would have freaked out."

We stayed there for a few days. It was beautiful, relaxing, and very rural. Every morning we'd sit on the porch enjoying the delicious breakfast the chef made for us. Everything was fresh.

After breakfast Michel would go to work, and later we'd walk to town to meet him. Michel would meet us at the main hotel, which overlooked the outdoor market in the middle of town.

In the afternoon, when he was done working, we'd go to the beach. The beach was beautiful. The water was turquoise, clear, and warm. The sand was white, and no one was there but us.

Since it was Mardi Gras, every night after dinner we'd walk into town and join the festivities. In the middle of town everyone joined the parade that snaked up and down each street. The women's dresses were colorful and festive. Some guys had guitars, others had bongos, and some had something that looked like a trumpet. Everyone was dancing. It was one big party. It was so much fun.

Michel suggested that we should go back to Port-au-Prince, where the "real" Mardi Gras was. This time we decided to fly. The airport was in the middle of a forest in an open area with a little hut and a couple of chairs. The runway was packed-down dirt.

As we were waiting for our plane, we saw some guy, about a hundred feet away, walking out of the woods. He looked like he was hurt. Michel and I went over to him. As we got close to him, we saw that his left arm was barely hanging on. He looked like he was in shock. He spoke in patois and told Michel that he was cutting through a farm, but the farmer thought he was trying to steal some vegetables or fruit and hacked his arm with a machete. We took him back to the hut and Mary found some rags to wrap around his arm. It wasn't much help, but there was nothing else we could do. Unfortunately, since there wasn't a phone there, we couldn't call for a doctor. He thanked us, and minutes later, he walked away as our plane arrived.

When we landed, Thierry was there to pick us up and bring us to his house. During dinner, Michel and Thierry told us about the Mardi Gras parade that we were going to after dinner.

We all climbed into Thierry's car and drove to a neighborhood that was close to where the parade would be passing. Michel suggested that we write down the address where we parked. He said, "Something might happen, and we might get separated. Sometimes these parades get dangerous, and people get shot." We might get shot?

He said, "There are three groups of security: the police, a separate security group, and the Tonton Macoute." The Tonton Macoute were created by Papa Doc and then supported by his son Baby Doc. They were very violent and could do whatever they wanted, especially when it came to crowd control. Michel said, "Citizens of Haiti don't have human rights."

The girls and I decided to stay as close to Michel and Thierry as we could. If they started running, we'd start running. When we got to the parade, there were hundreds of people lining the streets. Everyone was in a festive mood, cheering, singing, and dancing. The women were gorgeous and dressed in their best party dresses. All of us started dancing.

Some people who were dancing had a baby bottle, filled with what I assume was some type of liquor, hung around their necks with a long string tied to the neck of the bottle. It was an ingenious idea. If they got thirsty while they were dancing, they had their drink ready and didn't worry about spilling it.

About an hour later, we heard something that sounded like a firecracker, but it wasn't. About thirty yards from us we saw a couple of people fall to the pavement. Everyone started running. As we were running, we heard several more shots. It was pandemonium with everyone running in all directions.

Thank goodness Michel had prepared us for this. The girls and I were stuck like glue to Michel and Thierry. We got back to the car, caught our breath, and decided it might be safer to go to a local bar.

We stayed in Port-au-Prince for one more day and then returned to New York City.

Drawing of the main market across from the hotel

Waiting for the *Arthemise* to depart

The *Arthemise*

On the crowded deck of the *Arthemise*

Drawing on the beach in Jeremie

Twenty-four
New York City Marathon

1978

One Saturday morning my friend Peter, who I played softball with, called me and asked if I wanted to go uptown and run in a 10k race in Central Park. He said, "After the race we'll have breakfast downtown at one of those delis on Second Avenue. Their cheese blintzes are delicious."

We took the Lexington Avenue subway up to 86th Street and walked over to the park. The race was starting at the 90th Street entrance.

I thought that I was in good enough shape to run 6.2 miles. If I paced myself, it wouldn't be a problem. Peter felt the same way. But I was wrong. I was exhausted when I finished and so was Peter.

As we were walking to the subway, he asked me, "Do you think you could run a marathon…the New York City Marathon?"

I didn't even know what a marathon was.

He said, "It's a 26.2-mile race, in the fall, that goes through the five boroughs."

I told him, "I don't think so, but maybe if I trained for it I could."

He bet me a breakfast that I couldn't. It wasn't a bad bet for him since I didn't have any idea what kind of training it would take to get in shape to do that.

The next day I kept thinking about it and decided that I'd sign up for it. After work I went downtown, filled out an application, and got my number. It was that simple. There were about 10,000 runners that year. Today they have over 50,000 runners and over 100,000 applicants.

Although I wasn't sure how to train for a marathon, I figured if I ran a couple of miles each day, six times a week, increasing my mileage little by little, that that would be enough. I had four months to get in shape.

The only sneakers I had were black Converse sneakers. I figured I needed running sneakers, but I couldn't afford real ones which cost over fifty dollars. Then one day, as I was walking down Broadway after running in Central Park, I saw a store on 50th Street that was selling sneakers that looked like the real thing but only cost $9.99. I wasn't sure how good they were, but they looked like running sneakers and I could afford them. They fit well. I trained all summer with them and ran the marathon without any foot problems.

After work, I'd go home, change, and go over to the West Side Highway, which was still elevated, and run a couple of miles. On weekends I'd run several miles around the Lower East Side, Chinatown, the Wall Street area, and Battery Park.

As it got closer to the race, the weather got colder, and the days got darker earlier, which made training a lot less fun. Besides the challenge of training, it was a challenge to stay healthy.

The night before the race, my friend Tony, who had a car, said, "I'll drive you to the start of the race at the Verrazano Bridge if you want." Of course I did, so the night before, he slept at my place. I made dinner, and early the next morning, he dropped me off. I was excited and also nervous. Even though I had trained to the best of my ability, I didn't know if I could run 26.2 miles. It was a beautiful October day but unusually warm. By the end of the race it was over seventy degrees. I liked running in warm weather, so I didn't think it would bother me, but then again, I had never run 26.2 miles in the heat. After the race a lot of people were complaining about the heat, so after a few years, the New York Road Runners club moved the race to November when it's cooler.

Running over the Verrazano Bridge was exhilarating, and the view was spectacular.

As we ran through each street in each borough, there were crowds of people cheering us on. In some areas the people were eight-deep.

I couldn't believe I was running in a world-class sporting event. Everyone was in a good mood. I was doing well, but after twenty-three miles, I hit the wall. It's a condition that usually happens to men and is caused by the depletion of glycogen stored in your muscles, causing sudden fatigue, loss of energy, and illogical thinking. I had heard about this and was hoping it wouldn't happen to me, but it did. Suddenly I started thinking that maybe I should stop running and walk to build up my energy so that I could finish the race. I knew that if I gave into this feeling, I would probably never finish the race, so I fought through it and continued to run. What an unusual feeling.

I knew the race was almost over when we entered Central Park at 90th Street and Fifth Avenue. I suddenly got a burst of energy, and when I exited the park at 59th Street, by the Plaza, the feeling was euphoric. Running up Central Park South through a gauntlet of people ten to fifteen deep on either side and the sound of the cheering were overwhelming.

I finished in 4:35:35 and in 7,200th place. The numbers didn't matter. All that mattered was that I finished. I'll never forget the feeling of crossing the finish line, receiving a medal, and wrapping myself in the tin-foil blanket.

What a great opportunity to experience this. The temperature was 75 degrees when I finished, a beautiful fall day. On the way home several people asked me if I had won. In fact, I was in Queens when the winners, Bill Rodgers and Greta Waitz, crossed the finish line. When I got back to my loft, I turned on the TV to watch the news and the marathon that I was part of.

The next day, in spite of my legs aching, I went to work to tell everyone how I did, since several of them went through the summer hearing about my training.

I also called Peter the next day to tell him he owed me a breakfast.

October 22, 1978
Sponsored by:
Manufacturers Hanover
Rudin Family
Perrier
New York Telephone
New Times

The New York Road Runners Club Certifies that

Weldon R. Clears

has completed the full 26 mile 385 yard marathon footrace

Meet Director

Mayor of the City of New York

Time 4:35:35 Place 7200

New York City Marathon '78

Run for the Samuel Rudin Trophy

Twenty-five
Tidbits

Tattoo in Provincetown

I was visiting Steve one day, and he asked me, "Do you want to go to Provincetown for a few days and visit some of my friends with me?"

I had never been there, and since I had plenty of vacation time, I said, "Why not?"

The next week I rented a car and picked him up. We were going to stay at the house of his friend Caroline, who lived with three other women. I didn't know anything about Provincetown, so on the way up, Steve told me, "It's an artists' town, and most of the people who live there are gay," which didn't matter to me.

Caroline and her friends were nice and said we could stay there. During the day we'd sit around talking or walk around town. The stores and bars were very cool. Many of the stores had clothing and jewelry made by people who lived there.

One night after dinner we were all sitting in the living room drinking and smoking a joint. Caroline, who had small tattoo dashes that surrounded her mouth and eyes like Vali Meyers, the

Witch of Positano, who was her friend, asked me, "Do you want me to give you a tattoo?"

I had never thought about getting a tattoo, so I said maybe. As I was thinking about whether I should get one, several of the other people in the room said, "Getting a tattoo from her is special and will bring you good luck."

Since I could always use good luck, I said yes.

Instead of asking me what I wanted, she said that she would know what design to give me by the vibe she was getting from me. She only asked me where I wanted it.

I told her, "On the back of my right shoulder."

She went to her room and returned with a sewing kit. She tied three sewing needles together and then took out a bottle of India ink.

I took off my shirt, and after about an hour she was done. I couldn't wait to see it. It looked like a little sun, which was amazing because there weren't many things she could have drawn that could make me feel better than the sun. I loved the summer and the warmth of the sun. She nailed it, and I think my luck got better.

We stayed there for another couple of days. One morning, one of the girls and I watched the sunrise, and that night we went to the same spot and watched the sunset. It's one of the unusual things you can experience in Provincetown.

Dancing

I always liked dancing. When I was in elementary school, I always had fun square dancing although I was shy, and picking a girl to dance with was never easy. But when I was thirteen, I won a twist contest at a party. The contest involved couples doing the twist with a balloon tied to each boy's ankle. While dancing you tried to step on the other guy's balloon and pop it.

We won, and she gave me a big hug and a kiss. From that point on I was hooked. I even thought that I was good at dancing.

Several years later when I was at a club with Gail, we danced to one of the band's songs. She danced the Lindy really well. After we finished dancing, she asked me, "Would you like me to show you how to do the Lindy?" I guess I wasn't as good as I thought.

The next night I went over to her apartment, and she showed me some moves. She said that if I wanted to practice, I could use a wooden chair, just like the warden said in the song, "Jailhouse Rock:" "Hey, buddy, don't you be no square. If you can't find a partner, use a wooden chair." Gail also said, "You can also practice by using a doorknob. Pretend that the doorknob is a girl's hand."

The rest of the week I practiced every night, and to my surprise it helped, and I got better.

One night, after watching the movie *Shall We Dance*, with Ginger Rogers and Fred Astaire, I decided that I'd like to dance like Fred. He made it look so easy.

The next day, I decided to take tap dance lessons. The only place I could think of that might give tap lessons was Carnegie Hall. So, after work, I went there and was told a class in tap was starting the next week. I signed up for ten lessons. I tried my best and found that tap dancing was a lot harder than Fred made it look.

After several weeks, I asked my teacher if I should buy tap shoes, but she said, "Why don't you wait, honey?" I was a little disappointed because I wanted to sound like everyone else when we did line dancing. After the group of ten lessons ended, I again asked my instructor whether I should get tap shoes. Again she said that maybe I should wait.

I thought that the instructor was trying to tell me something about my dance ability, so I decided not to waste any more money. It was a fun experience, but I didn't think tap was my thing.

The New Emigrants

One night Gail's cousin Janis and her boyfriend, Harry, and I decided that we were going to create an underground talk show. My fantasy was to get our show on PBS. Our format was to interview new up-and-coming artists in my loft. My friend John had video equipment, and he'd tape it for us.

We did four tapings. Our first taping was of us introducing ourselves to our audience. The first interview was with Judy Nylon, who was a widely influential multidisciplinary artist who was in the group Snatch. The interview went well. She was open, informative, and entertaining.

The second interview was with Ruth Marten, a fine arts painter and commercial illustrator, who was into cosmetic art. She used tattooing and scarring as a way to express herself. She said, "Skin is my canvas." The subject matter was different, interesting, and nothing that I had ever heard of.

The third and last interview was with Charles Stettler, who had just come to America from Switzerland and wanted to live in NYC. It was interesting to hear what someone from another country, with no money, coming to New York City, expected and hoped for.

The interviewees were different, and the show had potential. The give-and-take between them and us worked well. For some reason, after filming these interviews, we stopped. We never interviewed anyone else, and I never presented the videos to PBS. I should have. They were raw and basic with no pretense.

The Senders

Steve and I were hanging out in his loft on Tenth Street between Avenues C and D one day, and he said, "My band is going to rehearse this afternoon." I was going to leave but he asked me, "Do want to join us?" He knew that I played a Hammond B3 organ and had heard me play. Since he had rented a stand-up piano, he said I could play that.

The Senders were one of my favorite bands, and to have a chance to play with them was something I couldn't pass up. Philippe was a good lead singer, handsome, and a perfect front man. Steve, Wild Bill, and Tony Machine were all good musicians and had a great stage presence.

The whole time I was playing I kept imagining I was Dylan playing the upright piano when he was recording songs for *Highway 61 Revisited.*

Johnny Thunders

I met Johnny when he lived with his mom in Queens. Then he was Johnny Genzale and was going out with Gail's cousin Janis. Some nights, on our way to CBGB or Max's Kansas City we'd pick him up. Sometimes when he wasn't ready, we'd go upstairs to his mom's apartment and wait for him in his room. I knew he was Italian the first time we picked him up because his mom's apartment smelled like my house did on a Sunday afternoon when my mom was making tomato sauce. Several times he wasn't ready because he was either practicing or trying to figure out what to wear and had lost track of time. One night I asked him why he practiced so much, and he said, "I wanna get into a band," which he did. First the New York Dolls and then the Heartbreakers and then on his own. Johnny was talented, always dressed sharply, and had a special, magnetic personality. Most of all, he was nice guy.

Meeting Muhammad Ali

I was very lucky to sort of meet Muhammad Ali three times. Each time I met him was a thrill.

The first time was when I lived in Miami Beach, which I mentioned in my Miami Beach story.

The second time I met him was one night when Steve and I were walking down 7th Avenue, going to the Peppermint Lounge. We saw a big crowd at the entrance to the Sheraton Hotel on 53rd Street and 7th Avenue, so we went over to see what was going on. Muhammad Ali was signing autographs. It was exciting seeing the champ again. Like everyone else, we also wanted to get his autograph, but the only piece of paper I had in my wallet besides money and my driver's license was my draft card, which he signed. Too bad I lost it.

The third time I met him was at his training camp in Pennsylvania. I went with my friend Tim White, who was interviewing him for *Rolling Stone* magazine.

Conclusion

I hope you've enjoyed these stories. It was an amazing time. I still live in New York City, and my life has continued to be interesting, challenging, and wonderful. I got married in 1984 and have enjoyed the fun and adventures of being a husband to Patti Kantor and a father to Amanda and Allison. In 2001 I invented and got a patent for a device that reduces the pain of lateral epicondylitis (tennis elbow). It's called Elbow Ease, https://www.elbow-ease.com.

I'm a lucky guy to have met some great people, friends that I still have, and to have experienced some things that I never thought I would.

Loves of my life: Amanda, Patti, and Allison

Made in United States
North Haven, CT
23 April 2022

18504592R00109